FOUR SUPER GAY PLAYS

Attack of the Killer Bs

Bitches

L.A. Tool & Die: Live!

Camp Killspree

P L A Y S T O O R D E R

A Plays to Order collection
Published by Plays To Order
5724 Hollywood Blvd., Suite 109
Los Angeles, CA 90028
www.playstoorder.com

First Edition: February 2016

ISBN-13: 978-0692627419
ISBN-10: 0692627413

CREDITS:

Plays to Order logo, *Bitches* logo, *L.A. Tool & Die: Live!* logo and poster/postcards by Mike Ross
L.A. Tool & Die: Live! poster photography by Jay Lawton
L.A. Tool & Die: Live! production photos by Sean Abley
Attack of the Killer Bs photos by Patricia Sutherland
Attack of the Killer Bs poster by Sean Abley
Bitches (1993) photos by Brian McConkey
Bitches (1995) photo by Jennifer Girard
Bitches (2014) photos by Brandon Clark/ The Magnum Players
Bitches (1993) program cover by Sean Abley
Camp Killspree photos by Roger Lewin/Jennifer Girard Studio

FOUR SUPER GAY PLAYS

Attack of the Killer Bs

Bitches

L.A. Tool & Die: Live!

Camp Killspree

By
Sean Abley

PLAYS TO ORDER

OTHER PLAYS BY SEAN ABLEY

From Playscripts, Inc.

The Adventures of Rose Red (*Snow White's Less-Famous Sister*)
Bad Substitute
Dracula's Daughters: A Family Comedy
Dr. Frankincense and the Christmas Monster
End of the World (*With Prom to Follow*)
Reefer Madness

From Brooklyn Publishers

Double Trouble On The Prairie
Elevator Games
Exposed! Eight 10-Minute Scenes About What Really Happened
Historically Bad First Dates
Horror High
Horror High: The Musical
Most Popular Kid In School
Princess Inchworm Measures The Ocean
Two-Faced: A Tragedy...Sort Of
We Wish You A Merry Spendmas!
What Would Happen If...? Eight Tales of Improbability

From Eldridge Plays and Musicals

The RISE of the House of Usher

<u>DEDICATION</u>

To everyone at the Factory Theater in Chicago, IL, 1992-1997, where I lived, learned to write, and had the most artistically fulfilling five years of my life.

And to the late Joey Meyer, the original "Kevin" in *Attack of the Killer Bs*, "Carmelle" in *Bitches*, "Rose" in *Camp Killspree*, my roommate, my co-conspirator, and my best friend. I still miss you every time I write a play.

TABLE OF CONTENTS

Forward

Introduction

FORWARD

Dear Person Reading This,

FACT: You are going to have the time of your life performing the plays of Sean Abley.

Seriously! You're going to have a super-awesome experience. You will look ridiculous. You will say and do things that are wildly inappropriate and offensive. You will dance. You will murder and/or be murdered. You will lie, cheat, and steal while murdering. You will dance some more. You might end up in prison or on the cheerleading squad. There will be LOTS of blood. And profanity. Also, nudity. And there will be more blood.

Everything in the world that's wildly inappropriate, irreverent, satirical, offensive, and shockingly hilarious can be found in the pages of a Sean Abley play. And you, Person Reading This, are LUCKY because you get a chance to perform all of it.

But here's the thing: you gotta put ALL of yourself into a Sean Abley play. You must pour your guts, your heart, your soul, and your willingness to be dangerous, bold, and vulnerable into every single choice or it won't work. And you're gonna want it to work because the audience will ADORE you for your bravery.

Wait—being brave is important for a Sean Abley play?! YES. Trust me. I've been chased by zombies, homicidal maniacs, and pod people. I've confronted evil prison wardens. I've sung gleefully about murder and setting fire to an orphanage. I've been punched, slapped, and chased by a 50-foot woman. And I got to do some of the punching and slapping! I was exhausted after every performance because Sean's writing asked me to put every fiber of myself into every choice. And I loved every second of it.

So put on your sassy-pants. Take a large dose of "I don't care how ridiculous I look." Add two enormous scoops of "extreme willingness to accept laughter from an audience." Crack open a Sean Abley play. Shake vigorously. Enjoy!

Amy Seeley
Playwright-Director
Co-Founder, Factory Theater
Incredibly Famous Person*

*Really.

INTRODUCTION

Wow! Thank you, Amy Seeley! I sound amazing!

But I wasn't always so incredible. My first produced play was terrible. T-e-e-r-r-r-ible. Like, unsalvageable. Trust me, I was going to do a "polish" (fancy word for rewrite) on it for this collection, and that turd refused to shine. *Corpse Grinders*, adapted from the Ted V. Mikels exploitation film of the same name, and directed by my boyfriend at the time, was an unqualified bomb. "Gross, misogynistic and unnecessary..." began the review by Achy Obejas of the Chicago Reader. "I was stunned by the sheer worthlessness of it all" was her parting shot. This was 1990. And she was right! Who did I think I was?!

Reefer Madness (non-musical, a decade earlier, I WAS THERE FIRST!!!) came next, and it was a big hit. Yay! And out of that came the core of the Factory Theater, founded in 1992. Amy was a part of that, and together with a group of friends we started a theater company in a storefront in the Rogers Park neighborhood of Chicago. Hey Amy, remember that time we heard gunshots outside during rehearsal and the cops came and searched the theater? Crazy.

Attack of the Killer Bs was the first play to bring big audiences to the Factory. We needed a new play after our first two shows bombed, so over the Christmas break in 92 I spent four days cranking out a script while house sitting for a friend. Oh, did I mention I was living in the basement of the Factory at that time? Yeah, so house sitting was awesome because there was heat. Two months later we opened and had our first sell out show at the Factory.

Bitches was written in large part for the original cast. By this point we'd been doing *Killer Bs* for months and needed something new. After twelve days of rehearsal (yes, that's right) and a few dance rehearsals for the cheerleading routines, we opened to rave reviews. Phew! Our laziness paid off again! Sadly, *Bitches*'s success would be the beginning of the end of our time in our first home—someone called the fire marshal after attending one of our sold out performances, the city got involved, and The Man began the slow and steady process of driving us out of our storefront. (Spoiler: The Factory just celebrated its twenty-somethingth anniversary, so it all turned out okay.)

We eventually moved *Bitches* to Bailiwick Repertory, where David Zak was the Artistic Director. He asked me to write something for the Pride Performance Series, the LGBT festival that was basically *the* place for gay theater in Chicago. I don't remember if David was the one who suggested a gay slasher play, but considering what a huge horror movie fan I am, it makes sense that either I came up with the idea, or someone would think I was the perfect person to write that kind of script.

As per usual, I cranked out the first draft really quickly, anticipating adding material as we rehearsed. About a year earlier Rick Beech (who would play "Andrew" in the original production) and I had been hanging out and I saw a Dominos Pizza flyer announcing their new "Sausage Feast!" I remember saying at the time, "That sounds like a great name for a gay play…" Rick brought that up constantly for months, so when it came time to write *Camp Killspree*, the original name was *Sausage Feast*. (An apt title considering the amount of nudity in the script.)

I wouldn't revisit naked gay theater for another couple decades, this time at the behest of Michael Shepperd, Artistic Director of Celebration Theatre in Los Angeles. (I'd moved to L.A. to work in The Industry.) He wanted a late-night show, I said, "Hey, why don't I adapt a gay porn?" and he said, "Yes!" Celebration got seven sold out weeks of *L.A. Tool & Die: Live!*, adapted from the adult film by Joe Gage. I'd like to credit my subtle and nuanced writing, but I'm guessing the cast of eight guys with big penises who spent about 75% of the show with their dicks out probably helped.

I hope this collection is, if nothing else, an enjoyable read. These plays were a blast to write, a joy to perform, and (I hope) fun to watch. I mostly write for kids these days (shhhhh, don't tell their teachers!), but these shameful relics of my sordid past are dear to my heart. If anything strikes your fancy, please let me know—I'd love to hear what you think (and/or have a good five-star review or two on Amazon...)

Sean Abley
Los Angeles, CA
2016

Me in *Attack of the Killer Bs*, Factory Theater West, Los Angeles, 1999. Yes, I did this to myself.

ATTACK OF THE KILLER B'S

A killer one-act comedy by

Sean Abley

Attack of the Killer Bs, original poster art, Factory Theater, Chicago IL, 1993

Attack of the Killer Bs, Factory Theater, 1993
Lori Lee, Kristen Swanson, Marssie Mencotti, Renee Williams Hense, Amy Seeley

Attack of the Killer Bs cast, Factory Theater, Chicago 1993

Attack of the Killer Bs Los Angeles cast, Factory Theater West, 1999

<u>ACKNOWLEDGEMENTS</u>

Attack of the Killer B's was first performed at the Factory Theater, Chicago, IL on February 26th, 1993 in repertory with *Reefer Madness*. The production was directed by Sean Abley and Amy Seeley and stage managed by Jenn Seal and Bo Blackburn. Fight choreography by Kirk Pynchon. Makeup by Jill Rothamer. The cast was as follows:

GLEN / GLENDA..Sean Abley
BARBARA..Amy Seeley
ZOMBIE #1, POT PARTY GUEST, PRISON GUARD, MILES,
    BRIAN...Scott Parkinson
BEN, HARRY #2, COP, CHUCK....................................Jim Blanchette
HARRY, RALPII, BURNT MANIAC.............................Jesse Dienstag
TOM, BILL, PRISON GUARD, KEVIN........................ .....Joey Meyer
JUDY, BLANCHE, BARTOWSKI.............................Marssie Mencotti
HELEN, MAE, DUTCH, MARIANNE........Renee Hense née Williams
KAREN, ALLISON, DIANE........................Jenny Laffey née Kirkland
ZOMBIE #2, JACK, GO-GO DANCER, NORMAN,
    MICHAEL..................................... ....Kirk Pynchon
VIVIAN, BENNI, MRS. VOORHEES.. ....Lori Lee
LOUISE, MARION, THEODORA, MICHEL.......... ..Kristen Swanson
BARBARA'S MOM, UNDERSTUDY..............................Jill Rothamer
TOWNSPERSON W/LINE, UNDERSTUDY....................Bruce Green
SHAPE, UNDERSTUDY..Michael Beyer
ENSEMBLE, UNDERSTUDY..Brad Fridell

EXTRA SPECIAL THANKS TO: Jeff Rogers for his original direction of the *Reefer Madness* section, Mike Meredith for mucho audio assistance, Marssie Mencotti for all the word processing, Jim Hense for his video help. The *Reefer Madness* company, George Romero, Alfred Hitchcock, Wes Craven, Louis Gasnier, Don Siegel and all other B- movie directors.

Attack of the Killer Bs, Factory Theater, Chicago 1993
Amy Seeley (Barbara), Sean Abley (Glen/Glenda), Joey Meyer (Kevin)

CHARACTERS

GLEN / GLENDA – Mid twenties, dressed from the late 60's
BARBARA – Glen/Glenda's sister, mid twenties, dressed late 60's
BEN – Thirtyish, 1960's
HARRY – late thirties, grouchy, 1960's
HELEN – late thirties, Harry's skittish wife, 1960's
TOM – a nice boy, 1960's
JUDY – Tom's girl, 1960's
KAREN – Harry and Helen's daughter, teens, 1960's
JACK – 1930's drug dealer
MAE – same, seen better days, 1930's
BLANCHE – woman of loose morals, 1930's
BILL – innocent teen, 1930's
RALPH – drug crazed dope addict, 1930's
HARRY #2 – no good, cheatin' dope fiend, 1930's
VIVIAN – Harry #2's girlfriend, 1930's
ALLISON – Harry #2's wife, 1950's
COP – a cop, 1930's
BARTOWSKI – female prison warden, inappropriately sexy, 1970's
DUTCH – masculine female inmate, 1970's
BENNI – female inmate, Dutch's "friend", 1970's
LOUISE – nice girl inmate, 1970's
BURNT MANIAC – possibly with fingerknives and felt hat
FEMALE GUARDS – two female prison guards
BARBARA'S MOM – perfect mother, 1950's
NORMAN – mid thirties, odd, hotel manager, 1960's
MARION – mid thirties, cool blonde with a secret, 1960's
MILES – any age, conspiracy theorist, 1960's
THEODORA – any age, emotionless, 1960's
TOWNSPERSON – someone who needs a line, 1960's
KEVIN – hero, contemporary
BRIAN – any character from a slasher film, 1980's
MICHAEL – ditto   CHUCK – ditto
MICHELE – ditto
DIANE – ditto
MARIANNE – ditto
SHAPE – hulking killer, possibly in a hockey mask
MRS. VOORHEES – doting mother, 1980's
VARIOUS ZOMBIES AND TOWNSPEOPLE

NOTE ON DOUBLING: The original cast list is a good guide for doubling, but obviously this could be changed around, or the larger roles could be distributed more evenly, which would make some of the quick changes much easier. (Particularly tough – "Michael" to "Norman" in the final scene.)

SETS, PROPS AND LIGHTING

We accomplished what we needed for the original Chicago production, and the subsequent Los Angeles production, with two chairs, two benches and five entrances on a unit set (we also made entrances from the house) and a ton of easy to find, or make, props. Our "Theater for $5" aesthetic allowed us to create and buy props that looked as cheap as they cost. Lighting was used to suggest scene/location changes, along with chair and bench placement.

Scene changes should be made by the actors moving the chairs, benches, etc., as naturally as possible as the lights change and actors move from one location to another. There should be NO blackouts in the production except for the very end. This keeps the pace quick – the original production clocked in at fifty minutes without an intermission.

SOUND

The original production used tons of sound cues, including a musical "score" during the chase scenes and transitions. This helped us create a "film" onstage.

COSTUMES

If you want to follow a strict film color scheme, I would suggest:

Scene One – 1960's, Black and white (so the blood shows up better!)
Scene Two – Ditto
Scene Three – 1930's, Black and white except Allison in 1950's, full color.
Scene Four – 1970's, full color
Scene Five – Same, except Barbara's Mom in 1950's, and the Burnt Maniac in 1980's.
Scene Six – 1970's, full color
Scene Seven – carry over from Scene Six
Scene Eight – 1960's, Black and white
Scene Nine – 1960's, Black and white
Scene Ten – 1980's, full color

However, that's a lot of black and white. In the original production the only black and white scene was Scene Three.

ONE MORE THING

Keep the last scene of the teens in the cabin loose. Our cast had a great time improvising during this scene, which fleshed it out in a fun way.

ATTACK OF THE KILLER Bs

By Sean Abley

Scene One

(*GRAVEYARD. LATE 1960'S. BARBARA and GLEN enter, bickering.*)

GLEN. They're coming to get you, Barbara!

BARBARA. Shut up, Glen!

GLEN. (*Mocking:*) Shut up, Glen. What's the matter? Scared?

BARBARA. Stop it! You are so ignorant!

GLEN. I'm ignorant? Who's scared of the cemetery?

BARBARA. I am not scared of the cemetery.

GLEN. (*Mocking:*) I am not scared of the cemetery. Then why are your hands shaking? They're coming to get you, Barbara!

BARBARA. Would you please shut up?! Have some respect, for goodness sake.

GLEN. For what? That old bitch? No way.

BARBARA. Glen! She's our mother!

GLEN. And she's dead, Barbara. What little respect I had for her while she was alive, which wasn't much, I buried out here with her when she croaked. And if you were smart you'd do the same thing.

BARBARA. Fine.

GLEN. I can't believe you still let her control you this way. Wherever she is, she's too busy shoveling hot coals to know you're out here in the friggin' rain paying your "respects." (*She waves him off, kneels by the tombstone and crosses herself. Glen pulls out a cigarette and lights up.*)

BARBARA. At least move down wind.

(*He gives her a look, then moves. In the distance ZOMBIE #1 appears, shuffling toward them.*)

GLEN. Look, Barbara, here they come now. They're coming to get you, Barbara! Mother sent someone for you!

BARBARA. (*Fierce whisper:*) Shush! Leave the poor man alone. He'll hear you!

GLEN. (*Whisper:*) So sorry. (*Shouts:*) Hey! Over here! She's over here, gimpy!

BARBARA. That's it! I'm leaving. You bastard! (*BARBARA heads straight for ZOMBIE #1.*) I'm so sorry. Please don't listen to him. He doesn't –

(*ZOMBIE #1 attacks her, trying to take bites out of her flesh. They fight until GLEN steps in and yanks him off. GLEN and ZOMBIE #1 grapple, with the zombie repeatedly getting back up after he shouldn't. Finally ZOMBIE #1 pulls the tombstone out of the ground and bashed GLEN over the head with it, killing him. ZOMBIE #1 leans over and takes a huge bite out of GLEN, then drags his body away. ZOMBIE #2 appears and chases BARBARA, accomplished by both of them running/shuffling in place. ZOMBIE #2 shuffles closer, then further back, it's neck and neck until BARBARA finally breaks away and races to...)*

Scene Two

(FARMHOUSE. BARBARA dashes in and locks the door behind her.)

BARBARA. Poor Glen! *(She cries.)*

(OUTSIDE THE FARMHOUSE. BEN enters, fighting off a group of ZOMBIES. He fights his way to the door, but it is locked.)

BEN. Hello?! Anybody in there?! Open up in there! Open this damn door!

(BARBARA finally unlocks the door. BEN bursts in and slams it shut behind him.)

BEN. We gotta barricade this door! And these windows! They aren't very strong, but enough of them could break through just a regular door. You got any nails in this place? And wood. You got any wood? You got a hammer? Do you have any lumber? DO YOU HAVE A HAMMER?!
BARBARA. *(Bursts into tears.)* I DON'T KNOW!
BEN. You don't know? This is your house, ain't it? *(She shakes her head 'No.')* This ain't your house. Great. I'm sorry. Sorry. It's just that we gotta get it together and barricade the doors and windows or those...things... are gonna get in here. And then we're finished. Okay? *(She nods.)* Okay. You look through these drawers and stuff for nails and a hammer. I'm gonna go upstairs and pull the doors off the hinges. *(BEN turns to exit. BARBARA grabs him.)*
BARBARA. No!
BEN. It's okay. There aren't many of them out there yet. If anyone of them things comes near the house, you just holler. Okay? *(She nods.)* Okay.

(BEN exits. BARBARA looks around the house. Suddenly, HARRY steps out from the basement. He approaches her unseen until she turns around. She screams and fights him off as he tries to calm her.)

HARRY. No! Wait! It's okay! Shut up for a minute, will ya?! *(BEN rushes in, grabs Harry and starts beating him.)* Wait a minute, you idiot! I'm not one of those things! (*He struggles free.*) It's okay!

BEN. Sorry. Thought you were one of those...things.

HARRY. Well, I'm not one of those...things! I'm Harry Cooper. I got my wife and little girl with me, and a couple of kids we picked up along the way. My daughter, she's hurt pretty bad. Got bit by one of those...things.

BEN. Wait a minute. You said 'picked up' a couple of kids. You got a car?! Let's go! (*He races to the door, which he cautiously opens and looks for the car.*)

HARRY. Yeah, I got a car. What do you think, I'm an idiot? It's out of gas, genius.

BEN. Completely? The next town is only five miles away. We could make that on fumes!

HARRY. And what if we don't? My girl's hurt. She can't run. We'd never make it.

BEN. Then we'd leave you and her here and come back with help.

HARRY. Right! Like you'd come back after you got outta this trap. No way. We're staying down in the basement and the car stays put. Besides, a group of those...things... rolled it over off the road. It would take ten men to flip it back over.

BEN. (*He has moved away from the door, leaving it unlocked.*) In the basement? You've been here the entire time?

HARRY. Yeah, what about it?

BEN. You mean you didn't hear us screaming up here? We could've used some help up here, Cooper!

HARRY. How did we know what was going on up here? House coulda been full of those...things.

(*ZOMBIE #3 bursts in the unlocked door. HARRY cowers, using BARBARA as a shield, as BEN fights off the zombie and pushes it out the door. Once the zombie is out the door, HARRY runs up with the pretense of helping.*)

HELEN. (*Off.*) Harry? What's going on up there?

HARRY. Nothing, Helen. We'll be right down. Come on. Let's talk about this downstairs.

BEN. Uh uh. That place is a death trap. No way out. At least up here we got options. We'll use the basement as a last resort.

HARRY. You're outta your mind, mister! All these doors and windows? There's no way you could board all them up. I'm going downstairs.

BEN. Wait a minute! How do we know you'll let us in when we need it?

HARRY. (*Holds up the basement door keys.*) Once this door shuts, it ain't opening until the National Guard gets here.

BEN. Give me those keys, Cooper!

(*They fight. TOM and JUDY enter from the basement. They break up the fight.*)

TOM. Mr. Cooper, stop it! Stop it!

HARRY. This guy wants to kill us all!

JUDY. It's not that way, Mr. Cooper. We were listening downstairs. If we all work together we can board up the place and still have the basement if we need it.

TOM. So you see, Mr. Cooper, your plan is actually the best one. So we'll save it for last.

HARRY. (*Mulls this over, then:*) Helen! Get up here!

(*We hear HELEN's footsteps offstage as she comes upstairs – stomp, stomp, stomp, stomp – for a LOT of stairs. HELEN enters from the basement.*)

HELEN. Yes, Harry?

HARRY. We're gonna help secure the premises up here.

HELEN. Who are these people?

BEN. My name is Ben and this is –

BARBARA. Glen!

TOM. Glen?

BARBARA. He's still out there! One of those...things...attacked us and got Glen! We've got to go get him!

(*BARBARA bolts for the door. Everyone panics as BEN pulls her away.*)

BEN. We can't go out there now! We'll get help for Glen later.

HARRY. Yeah, right.

BEN. Shut up, Cooper! After we get out of here, we'll go get Glen. Okay?

BARBARA. (*Strong:*) Okay.

BEN. (*Stunned, impressed:*) Okay.

JUDY. Why don't we break up into teams?

BEN. Good idea.

HARRY. Helen, I want you to go back downstairs and watch after Karen.

HELEN. But Harry –

HARRY. Just do it! Somebody has to watch her and make sure she's alright. I'll be there if anything happens.

HELEN. Alright, Harry. (*She exits.*)

TOM. Let's get to work!

(*Everyone goes about securing the house. SHIFT FOCUS TO – BASEMENT. HELEN enters.*)

HELEN. Karen? Darling? (*KAREN appears behind her. Dead. Carrying a trowel.*) Karen, there you are...Karen...Karen...?

(*KAREN attacks HELEN, killing her with the trowel, then taking a bite out of her flesh. SHIFT FOCUS TO – UPSTAIRS.*)

HARRY. What was that? I heard a scream!

(*The ZOMBIES burst in, including KAREN and the now-zombified HELEN from the basement, and GLEN. They take over the house, killing and dragging away Harry, Ben, Tom and Judy, leaving GLEN and BARBARA at a stand off.*)

BARBARA. Glen? Glen, speak to me!

(*GLEN attacks BARBARA, trying to take a bite out of her. After a struggle, BARBARA winds up and slaps him hard across the face.*)

GLEN. (*Shocked:*) Ow!
BARBARA. Just because you are one of the dead risen from the grave to feast upon the living doesn't mean you have to be so ornery!
GLEN. Sorry! Ow...
BARBARA. Now let's get out of here before it's too late.
GLEN. To where?
BARBARA. Someone said something about a town less than five miles from here.
GLEN. That would be Springwood, right next to Camp Crystal Lake!
BARBARA. Let's run! We've got to get help!

(*They exit. SHIFT FOCUS TO –*)

Scene Three

(*MAE'S HOUSE, LATE 1930'S. A big reefer party is about to take place. JACK enters.*)

JACK. Hey, everybody! Come on in!

(*Everyone bursts in loudly from all directions, in a party mood. JACK and MAE are the hosts. BLANCHE with BILL in tow, RALPH, VIVIAN and HARRY #2, among others, are the guests. Everyone is dressed in shades of black and white.*)

BLANCHE. Come, Bill. Don't just stand there. Oh, Mae, this is Bill. (*Knowing nod:*) He's "okay".
MAE. If he's "okay" with you, he's "okay" with me. (*She offers BILL a firm handshake.*)
BILL. Nice to meet you.
MAE. Likewise. (*BILL and BLANCHE circulate. MAE approaches JACK.*) Who's the new kid?
JACK. That's Bill. He's "okay." Blanche has got herself quite a yen for him.

MAE. Not bad. Didn't think Blanche had that much taste. You got the supplies?

JACK. (*Hands her a package of joints.*) Right here. Twenty reefer cigarettes. One for every joe and jane in the place.

MAE. Perfect! Your name might be Jack, but you're ace-high straight. (*To the crowd.*) Here we go! (*She begins to hand out reefer.*)

RALPH. Oh, Mae, don't forget about me!

MAE. Ralph, I could never forget about you.

(*Everyone except BILL laughs a bit too loud and hard. BILL is puzzled.*)

BLANCHE. (*Offering Bill a reefer.*) Here, Bill. If you want a good smoke, try one of these.

BILL. Um, no thank you.

BLANCHE. Oh. I thought you were a good sport. Of course, if you're afraid...

(*Party and music instantly stop. All eyes turn to BILL. Slowly, he takes the joint. Party and music resume.*)

BLANCHE. That's better! I know you'll like it. I know you will! Now, just take a puff...

(*BLANCHE lights a match. Party and music instantly stop. All eyes turn to BILL. BILL takes a puff and gets the giggles. Then RALPH laughs. Then BILL. The laughter builds until everyone is laughing hysterically. Laugh, laugh, laugh. BARBARA and GLEN burst in. Party and music instantly stop. All eyes turn to BARBARA and GLEN.*)

BARBARA. Hello. Could you help us please? We're in a lot of trouble.

MAE. Jack, I don't think they're from around here.

JACK. Quiet you! (*The party resumes. JACK moves over to BARBARA and GLEN.*) Sure, kids. Come on in. Make yourselves comfortable. Now, how deep are ya in?

GLEN. Pretty deep. We were attacked by ghouls from beyond the grave not five miles from here. We need to call somebody! The police...or the morgue... or the newspapers!

JACK. You're in deep alright. But we'll get you all the "help" (*Pats his pocket full of reefer*) you need.

CROWD. (*Knowing laugh from the crowd.*)

BARBARA. Thanks.

JACK. Why don't you two relax while we figure out what to do.

(*JACK moves away. RALPH sidles up to BARBARA.*)

RALPH. (*Indicating Glen*:) So, are you pinned to that joe?

BARBARA. His name is Glen. And no, he's my brother.

RALPH. (*Making his move.*) Good! I mean...a good guy. He seems like a stand up kinda guy.

BARBARA. He is.

RALPH. Hey, don't get me wrong. I'm just making conversation. (*Offering her a reefer*:) How about a smoke?

BARBARA. Why yes, I'd love one. How thoughtful.

(*She takes the joint. RALPH lights it for her. By this time GLEN has been given a joint as well, although neither of them realize what they're smoking. They take a puff. The laughing begins again. As it reaches its hysterical peak, ALLISON bursts in, hysterical. She is in full color, dressed in 1950's clothes.*)

ALLISON. Harry! Harry, where are you?!

BARBARA. (*Stoned*:) Harry was killed. He was eaten by my brother and the rest of the undead.

ALL. (*Big laughter.*) Ah ha ha ha ha!

ALLISON. What are you talking about?!

HARRY #2. I'm right here, darling. Now, what's the matter?

ALLISON. What's the matter? I'll tell you what's the matter. I'm almost killed, and then I find you here with her! (*Points to Vivian.*)

ALL. (*Laugh.*) Ha ha ha!

HARRY #2. Vivian is just a friend. We've discussed this. Now, darling, what's this about you almost getting killed?

ALLISON. I was driving down the highway when I see this bright light up ahead. As I get closer I see it's a large, glowing orb, or ship, or something. Something not of this earth! It blocked the path of the car, and when I got out, that's when I saw it. It was horrible!

HARRY #2. What? Saw what, darling?

ALLISON. The man! The giant man! He touched me! He reached out and scratched me! Look! (*Shows the scratch on her arm.*)

ALL. (*Laugh.*) Ha ha ha!

ALLISON. He's out there, Harry! Please! You've got to do something! (*Cries hysterically.*)

JACK. We can get you help, doll. All the "help" (*Pats the reefer in his pocket*) you need!

ALL. (*Laugh.*) Ha ha ha!

HARRY #2. I don't think she needs your kind of help, Jack. I think she needs to lie down.

MAE. Let's take her into my room.

(*HARRY #2 and MAE take ALLISON off, then reenter.*)

BARBARA. Glen, what is this place? They don't seem to be helping anybody.

GLEN. I know. And I feel awfully queer all of a sudden. What's in these cigarettes?

BARBARA. I don't know, but I think it's time we made a graceful exit and got some help.

(*BARBARA and GLEN start to leave, but VIVIAN and HARRY #2 are arguing in their path toward the door.*)

VIVIAN. Well, I think you should put her away. In the loony bin!

HARRY #2. Quiet down! Can't you see she's distraught? And it didn't help to see you here, all hopped up on reefer!

VIVIAN. Reefer, schmeefer! Sounds like ol' Harry-boy fell back in love with his wife!

ALL. Ooooohhh...

HARRY #2. (*Grabs Vivian by the shoulders.*) Not now! Stop it! You know the score. Once the will is settled...

(*SOUND: Destruction from outside. The room shakes. Everyone is jostled back and forth.*)

ALL. What's going on? What was that? Etc...

ALLISON. (*Off.*) HARRY!! I WANT MY HARRY!

BARBARA. Oh, my goodness! Where is that coming from?

ALLISON. (*Off.*) HARRY! WHERE IS HARRY?!

MAE. I think it's coming from outside!

(*SPLIT FOCUS between MAE'S HOUSE and OUTSIDE, where ALLISON has entered. She is now fifty feet tall, as evidenced by the dollhouse-sized replica of Mae's House she towers above. The crowd inside the house all look "out" the windows of the fourth wall to see ALLISON. Their movements are times to be in sync with ALLISON's destruction.*)

ALLISON. HARRY!

VIVIAN. She must be fifty feet tall!

ALLISON. WHERE ARE YOU, HARRY? I'VE COME FOR YOU!

(*ALLISON shakes the house to an fro. The party guests are tossed back and forth.*)

HARRY #2. You gotta hide me! Somebody hide me! She'll kill me!

JACK. Beat it, kid! You wanna get the rest of us killed, too?!

(*ALLISON shakes the house again. The party guests are tossed about.*

VIVIAN races out the front door. ALLISON reaches down and picks up "Vivian" [aka a doll dressed just like the actress playing "Vivian"] and menaces her.)

HARRY #2. Vivian! Allison, no! Put her down!

(ALLISON tosses "Vivian" behind her. She shakes the house again. As the guests are jostled, HARRY #2 is tossed toward the open front door. ALLISON reaches down into the house. HARRY #2 is "grabbed" by something outside the door and is yanked out. ALLISON lifts her hand, which is now holding "Harry #2." She menaces him for a moment, then bites his head off.)

ALL. (*Scream in terror and disgust:*) Nooo!

(ALLISON exits with the newly decapitated "Harry #2." SOUND: Sirens.)

MAE. She's getting away!

(A COP rushes in. All the party-goers except BARBARA slyly put away their joints.)

COP. We couldn't stop her before she...you know...but the National Guard should be able to bring her down.
BARBARA. Oh, officer, thank goodness you're here! It's been too awful! First, my brother, Glen, was turned into a walking zombie by the undead risen from the grave, and now that huge woman has murdered that poor man and his concubine, and no one will do anything to help us! Please! We just want to go home!
COP. Is that a joint in your hand? Undead my behind! You've been attacked by the evil marijuana, weed with roots in Hell! Excuse my language. The only place you're going is the big house! Come on!

(COP puts handcuffs on BARBARA and drags her out. The party goes wild – GLEN begs the COP not to take her, and the party guests chime in, pro and con, about her arrest. Finally the COP and BARBARA exit.)

JACK. Alright, everybody, scram! Beat it, see!

(ALL exit quickly except JACK and GLEN.)

GLEN. Wait, you have to help me! You got Barbara into this mess in the first place!
JACK. Beat it, kid. I got things to do.
GLEN. Wait! At least tell me where they're taking her.

JACK. To the state correctional facility where she belongs.

GLEN. Where is that? I don't even know where we are!

JACK. Jeez, kid. Ain't you from around here?

GLEN. No.

JACK. Go out this door, turn left, go down the road, turn left again, walk three miles then go south two blocks. Now amscray, kid! (*He exits.*)

GLEN. But wait! Come back! Great! Now what am I going to do? (*A beat.*) Waitaminute! It's so crazy, it just might work!

(*GLEN exits. SHIFT FOCUS TO—*)

Scene Four

(*WOMEN'S PRISON, 1970's. BARBARA is herded in with DUTCH, BENNI and LOUISE by the COP. WARDEN BARTOWSKI looks them over.*)

COP. Come on, move it! Get in there!

BARBARA / DUTCH / BENNI / LOUISE. Quit shovin'! I'm movin'! etc...

COP. All your's, Bartowski. Got some fresh meat, and (*re: Dutch and Benni:*) some old fish.

DUTCH. You son of a bitch!

(*DUTCH lunges at the COP, who throws her to the ground.*)

COP. Better watch it, Dutch, or you're gonna buy yourself some time in solitary. Oh, I forgot. You'd probably like some time in "the hole." Ah ha ha ha ha!

(*DUTCH lunges at the COP again, but BENNI and LOUISE hold her back. COP exits, laughing.*)

BENNI. Don't, Dutch! It's what they want!

LOUISE. Listen to Benni! You're not doing yourself any favors.

DUTCH. I'll get that stupid fuck! If it's the last thing I do.

BARTOWSKI. How touching. How sisterly of you to pull her back. Because we wouldn't want that lovely skin of yours to get all bruised up, now would we? Lookie, lookie. I've got all my favorites back. (*She moves down the row, using her police baton inappropriately on each inmate.*) Louise, truly a surprise. Of anyone, I thought you were headed for the "straight" and narrow. Benni, what is it this time? Arson? Armed robbery?

BENNI. (*Haughtily:*) Manslaughter.

BARTOWSKI. My, my! Moving up to the big leagues. Didn't think ya had it in ya. And Dutch. Apparently we had a little misunderstanding. You see, you had at least five more years left when you walked out of here last week. So sorry. But now we can get to know each other real well...

DUTCH. Cram it, Barf-owski! Ah, ha ha ha ha!

(*BARTOWSKI slams DUTCH in the gut, and a big prison catfight ensues. As BARTOWSKI and DUTCH scream at each other, the other women cheer them on. Finally BARTOWSKI pins DUTCH to the ground.*)

BARTOWSKI. I think you'd better apologize, Dutch, before I lose my temper!

DUTCH. (*Choking:*) Kiss...my...ass...

BARTOWSKI. Oh, I'll kiss much more than your ass before I'm through!

BARBARA. Stop it! You're hurting her! (*Everyone looks at BARBARA in disbelief.*)

BARTOWSKI. (*Incredulous:*) What?!

BARBARA. You're choking her! You're hurting her!

BARTOWSKI. Oh, I don't think so, dearie. See, Dutch and I got an understanding between us. I don't dish out more than she can take. Ain't that right, Dutch?

DUTCH. Yeah, sure...

(*BARTOWSKI releases DUTCH. She moves over to BARBARA.*)

BARBARA. Oh, okay.

BARTOWSKI. What's your name, precious?

BARBARA. Barbara.

BARTOWSKI. Barbara. And why are you here, honey? (*Puts her arm around BARBARA and walks her away from the other girls.*)

BARBARA. There's been a terrible mistake.

BARTOWSKI. No!

BARBARA. Yes! And I feel just awful about it.

BARTOWSKI. I'm sure you do. Let's see if we can get it straightened out, shall we?

BARBARA. Yes, please. The mistake was—

(*BARTOWSKI yanks BARBARA's head backwards by her hair.*)

BARTOWSKI. The only mistake you made was thinking I gave a crap! Cuz I don't, see? All I care about is keeping you low life scuz buckets behind bars until your bush turns gray! (*BARTOWSKI throws BARBARA to the ground.*) Now get your shit together! It's shower time!

BARBARA. In front of everyone else?

BARTOWSKI. Whatsamatter? Ain't you reached puberty yet?

(*BARTOWSKI, DUTCH and BENNI laugh uproariously. Two GUARDS [played by men with breasts, cop skirts, but no makeup or wigs] enter with a shower curtain. They hold each end, covering the girls from the neck down from the audience. The women disrobe and shower behind the curtain. As the scene plays out, BARTOWSKI strolls back and forth, watching.*)

BARBARA. She gives me the creeps, watching us like that.
LOUISE. Get used to it.
BARBARA. I'm Barbara.
LOUISE. (*Holds out her hand to shake.*) I'm Louise. Nice to meet you.
BARBARA. Uh, I'd rather not. I feel weird touching another girl while I'm naked.
LOUISE. Suit yourself.
BARBARA. What did she mean by she and Dutch have an "understanding?"
LOUISE. Believe it or not, Dutch really is Barfowski's favorite. They know each other, "biblically" if you know what I mean.
BARBARA. That's horrible! I mean, I could never...well, never...you know.
LOUISE. Don't knock it til you try it.
BARBARA. Louise! You haven't!
LOUISE. Well, no. But sometimes I think it might be easier just to give in and enjoy it. It's not like we're getting it from anywhere else.
BARBARA. Louise! Look what prison has done to you! You're a smart, pretty girl. And you've turned into a bitter, dirty-mouthed, sexual deviant! I hate prison!
BARTOWSKI. Lock down in half an hour! Towel off and get back to your cells!

(*BARTOWSKI and the GUARDS exit. The women get dressed and go to their cells – DUTCH and BENNI in one, LOUISE and BARBARA in another. They go to bed.*)

BARBARA. I'm so tired. I haven't slept since seven o'clock this morning.
BENNI. Quiet down in there!
LOUISE. Don't get on Dutch or Benni's bad side. Any enemy of theirs doesn't last long in here.
BARBARA. You mean they get out?
LOUISE. Yeah, in a box.
DUTCH. Hey! Cut the fucking slumber party, girlies! We're trying to sleep over here!
BARBARA. Sorry!
DUTCH / BENNI. (*Mocking:*) Sorry! Ah, ha ha ha ha!
BARBARA. I'm just going to close my eyes and think of Glen coming to get me out of this hell. Please hurry, Glen! I don't think I can last much

longer in here. (*She sleeps.*)

Scene Five

(*BARBARA'S MOM enters. She is the picture of the perfect 1950's TV housewife.*)

MOM. Barbara! Barbara, honey! Time to get up!

BARBARA. (*Sleepily:*) I don't want to go to school...

MOM. Oh, you don't have to go to school. I've made your favorite for breakfast! Blueberry pancakes!

BARBARA. Blueberry pancakes...(*Suddenly awake:*) Mom! Oh, my goodness! Mom! You're alive!

MOM. Of course I'm alive, darling! What a silly thing to say!

BARBARA. Mom, you've got to help me! I'm in prison! It's horrible and they're mean and it's all a big mistake!

MOM. Oh, the only mistake you made (*Suddenly vicious:*) was being born, you worthless bitch!

BARBARA. Mom!

MOM. What a waste of time you turned out to be, you stupid whore! I can't believe I dragged my ass all the way down here just to listen to you whine. Your father couldn't come because the sight of your ass makes him vomit! And don't bother calling home, because it burned down! Gotta run. I'm gonna go home and drink myself into a nice, alcoholic blackout. Oh, and another thing? You're adopted!! Ah ha ha ha ha!

(*MOM exits. BARBARA covers her eyes and cries.*)

BARBARA. I'm not adopted! I'm not, I'm not, I'm not – (*Jerks upright.*) What...? Oh, thank goodness. It was all a dream.

GLEN. (*Off.*) Barbara!

BARBARA. Glen!

GLEN. (*Off.*) Barbara!

BARBARA. Glen, where are you?

(*GLEN enters.*)

GLEN. I'm right here, Barbara!

BARBARA. What are you doing here?

GLEN. I came to get you out of here!

BARBARA. How?

GLEN. (*Holds up a large skeleton key.*) I have the key!

(*A scarred hand reaches in from offstage, grabs GLEN around the head and yanks him off. The air is filled with screams. Burnt hands, perhaps with finger knives, shoot in from all entrances, clawing at the walls.*)

BARBARA screams and screams. A BURNT MANIAC, perhaps in a striped sweater, felt hat and finger knives, enters.)

MANIAC. Annoying horror movie franchise catchphrase! Ah, ha ha ha ha!
BARBARA. (*Screams:*) Noooooooooooo!

(*The BURNT MANIAC disappears. BARBARA pulls on her cell bars. To her surprise they pull apart. She leaps out of her cell and tries to run, but her feet stick to the floor.*)

BARBARA. Stupid feet! Move!

(*BURNT MANIAC enters.*)

MANIAC. Another catchphrase!!
BARBARA. I don't understand! What does that mean?!

(*The BURNT MANIAC disappears. BENNI wakes up and walks out of her cell to BARBARA, not realizing she is also in the dream world.*)

BENNI. What's going on in here?
BARBARA. Benni! I don't know! It's horrible! Come on, we've got to get out of here!
BENNI. Yeah, right, outta the big house.
BARBARA. It's not the big house! You've got to listen to me –

(*BURNT MANIAC enters.*)

MANIAC. Yet another catchphrase!
BENNI. Back off, motherfucker!
MANIAC. Let's start with something smaller, like a hand off!

(*The BURNT MANIAC swipes at BENNI's hand, cutting it off. Blood flies everywhere. He and BENNI fight. BARBARA tries to help, but is thrown to the side. Finally, he kills BENNI and shoves her body back into her cell. He turns to BARBARA, backing her into her cell. Just as he's about to kill her, BARTOWSKI enters.*)

Scene Six

BARTOWSKI. Rise and shine, ladies!

(*The lights flip on and the BURNT MANIAC disappears.*)

BARBARA. (*Wakes up.*) Oh, my goodness! What happened?
BARTOWSKI. Come on, Dutch! Benni! Get your asses out of bed.

DUTCH. I'm up. Come on, Benni. (*Sees Dutch's dead body, screams.*) Aaaaaaahh!!

BARTOWSKI. What the hell?! Jeez, Dutch! Why did ya do it?

DUTCH. What? I didn't do it!

BARTOWSKI. Who else coulda done it? I don't see anyone else in your cell.

DUTCH. Are you nuts?

BARTOWSKI. And I thought you two were an item...

BARBARA. She didn't do it! I saw who did it! I saw!

BARTOWSKI. Shut up, princess! No way you coulda seen who done this.

BARBARA. But I did! It was a man! In a hat, and he was all scarred up. Burnt or something. He tried to get me first, but Benni got in the way!

DUTCH. See!

BARTOWSKI. See what? There's no way any man could get in here without my knowing about it. You're dreaming.

BARBARA. But I was dreaming! That's it! When I went to sleep he came to me in my dreams!

LOUISE. Girl, you're not doing yourself any favors.

BARTOWSKI. Listen to your girlfriend, sweetie pie. All I know is Dutch is gonna fry for this one for sure. Nice knowing ya, honey.

DUTCH. But I didn't do it! I swear!

BARTOWSKI. Guards! Take her to solitary!

(*Two FEMALE GUARDS enter and drag DUTCH away.*)

DUTCH. Get yer hands off me!

FEMALE GUARD. Move it, you murdering lesbian psychopath!

BARTOWSKI. Ta, ladies. Be sure to bring some wienies to the barbeque. (*Cracks herself up.*) Wienies to the barbeque! God, I'm funny! (*She exits.*)

BARBARA. I'm next! If I go to sleep, he'll get me! And then they'll blame you, Louise!

LOUISE. What?!

BARBARA. So you have to help me, or you're next. Either on the chair, or in your sleep!

LOUISE. Look, Barbara, there is no way someone can kill you in your sleep. You probably heard Dutch killing Benni subconsciously and incorporated it into your dreams.

BARBARA. Then how do you explain this! (*BARBARA shows LOUISE an impossibly small wound on her arm.*)

LOUISE. What?

BARBARA. This! (*A beat. Points.*) This! Right here! This wound! On my arm! How do you explain this?!

LOUISE. You did it to yourself. A classic case of self mutilation stemming from an inferiority complex compounded with paranoid delusions induced by incarceration. Easy.

BARBAR. Well, think what you want, but I'm not going to sleep until Glen comes to get me out.

(*BARTOWSKI enters.*)

BARTOWSKI. Your highness! You got a visitor. Your mother.

BARBARA. My mother? But my mother is –

BARTOWSKI. Get movin'. I ain't got all day, and you only got five minutes. Louise, get your ass down to Section C.

(*LOUISE exits. BARTOWSKI leads BARBARA to the visiting area. GLEN, dressed as their mother, enters.*)

GLEN. Darling, it's so nice to see you again. (*Big wink.*)

BARTOWSKI. How touching! Look, I'm cryin'. Oop. Sorry. Just got something in my eye. (*Cracks herself up.*) Just got something in my eye! Ya hear that one? God, I love me! Ah, ha ha ha ha! (*Exits.*)

BARBARA. Glen, what are you doing here?

GLEN. I'm here to get you out. I didn't want them to arrest me in hindsight, so I disguised myself.

BARBARA. Oh, Glen, I love you!

GLEN. I love you, too, Sis. I brought you something.

(*GLEN pulls out a calendar and hands it to BARBARA. [This calendar should have a pocket that hides a gun, and can hide the pieces of a gun from the next sequence.]*)

BARBARA. Uh, how thoughtful.

GLEN. It's marked on the day when I get you out of here.

BARBARA. Oh, Glen, but how?

GLEN. Like this.

(*GLEN forces a bullet out of his stomach and into his hand. BARBARA takes it.*)

BARBARA. One bullet?

GLEN. They'd never let me bring an entire gun in here, so I'll smuggle in all the pieces of one, then we'll put it together and blast our way out of here!

BARBARA. Do you think it will work?

GLEN. It has to. Just keep watching that calendar.

BARBARA. Goodbye!

GLEN. Goodbye! (*Exits.*)

(*MUSIC UP. LIGHT SHOW. DANCE MONTAGE. There are three focal points in this montage.*
1.LOUISE and a scantily clad male inmate GO-GO DANCER go-go dancing together.
2.BARTOWSKI, the COP and a FEMALE GUARD strap DUTCH onto the electric chair and execute her.
3.GLEN entering, vomiting up various pieces of the gun, handing them to BARBARA, then exiting.
The focus should shift back and forth between the three scenarios until DUTCH is dead and they drag her body off. GLEN then brings in the last piece of the gun. The MUSIC and LIGHT SHOW abruptly stop.)

GLEN. That's it.
BARBARA. Oh, Glen, I'm so scared!
GLEN. Me, too. But we gotta do what we gotta do. Here we go.

(*BARBARA, hiding the gun, drops to the floor in mock pain.*)

BARBARA. (*Bad acting.*) Oh, I'm sick! I'm so sick.
GLEN. Guard! Guard! Come quick!
BARTOWSKI. (*Enters.*) What do you want, you old bat?
GLEN. My daughter is sick. She needs medical attention.
BARTOWSKI. What she needs is a good kick in the teeth. Let me take a look.

(*BARTOWSKI moves closer to BARBARA. BARBARA whips out the gun.*)

BARBARA. Alright! Take it nice and easy. One false move and I'll...well, I'll blow your head off!
GLEN. Move it!
BARTOWSKI. You'll never get away with this! I'll see you both swing!
BARBARA. Shut up...princess!

(*BARBARA and GLEN drag BARTOWSKI off. Sirens are heard. MUSIC UP: Dead People Rising from the Grave. BENNI's corpse rises and staggers offstage. SHIFT FOCUS TO -- *)

Scene Seven

(*ON THE ROAD. BARTOWSKI enters, followed by BARBARA, still holding the gun, and GLEN.*)

BARBARA. Shall we kill her now, or take her with us and kill her slowly?
GLEN. Barbara! I'm sure I don't know what's gotten into you!
BARBARA. The joint's gotten into me!

GLEN. You've changed! I don't even know you any more! (*Cries.*)

BARBARA. Stop crying! We've got work to do. Move over there, Barfowski, and no funny stuff.

BARTOWSKI. I'll see you in Hell, you sniveling bitch!

BARBARA. (*Tough girl.*) Save me a table. (*She points the gun at BARTOWSKI.*)

GLEN. No!

(*GLEN jumps between BARBARA and BARTOWSKI just as she pulls the trigger. GLEN takes the bullet.*)

BARTOWSKI. You just shot your own mother!

BARBARA. (*Remorseless:*) He's already dead.

(*BARTOWSKI takes off running. BARBARA empties the gun in her direction.*)

BARBARA. Get back here!

GLEN. Barbara, stop it! Stop it!

(*They wrestle for the gun. GLEN wins.*)

BARBARA. Why'd you stop me? Now they'll find us!

GLEN. They'll find us anyway if we don't keep moving.

BARBARA. I'm sorry. It's just that prison did something to me. I have all this hate for society just boiling up inside of me.

GLEN. I know. I know. (*A beat.*)

BARBARA. Let's rest for a minute. (*They sit.*) Why don't you change into your real clothes?

GLEN. (*A beat.*) We need to have a talk. Barbara, in life, products are labeled accurately for easy identification. For example, if I were to open a can labeled "cherry soda," inside I would find a cherry soda. Likewise, if I were to open a can labeled "orange drink," inside I would find a cool, refreshing orange drink. But sometimes, at no one's fault, these labels get mixed up. Like mine. Barbara, I'm an orange drink in a cherry cola can. Remember when we were in prison just a minute ago? And you were in a cage? Well this body, this body with all of its facial hair and sexual organs, is my cage. And these clothes, these women's clothes, like that sweater of yours I admire so much, are like a furlough. A brief respite from the torture of being a woman trapped inside a man's body. Understand?

(*BARBARA considers this, then slowly removes the sweater she mysteriously acquired between prison and now, and hands it to GLEN.*)

GLEN. For me?

BARBARA. Yes. Whatever your label, Glen, I just want you to be happy.

GLEN. Thank you. I prayed you would understand. Now just...one more thing.

BARBARA. Yes?

GLEN. Could you call me...Glenda?

BARBARA. Glen...(*A beat, GLENDA sad face.*)...da. (*GLENDA happy face.*) I won't pretend finding out your brother is an undead transvestite is easy. But I want you to know I love you, no matter what.

GLENDA. I love you, too. (*They hug.*) Now let's get out of here before that warden tips off the authorities.

BARBARA. I see a light down the road.

GLENDA. Maybe it's a motel or something. We can hide out there til we come up with a plan.

(*They exit. SHIFT FOCUS TO -- *)

Scene Eight

(*MOTEL LOBBY, 1960's, black and white. NORMAN, the desk clerk, is checking in MARION, a cool blonde with a secret.*)

NORMAN. Here are your keys. (*He reaches for one set of keys, considers, then reaches for a different set.*) Would you like some help with your bags?

MARION. No. Thank you. I can manage.

NORMAN. Hungry? I could make some sandwiches?

MARION. No, I'm fine. Thank you.

NORMAN. Complimentary shower cap?

MARION. Oh, yes, thank you, I could use one.

NORMAN. Let me help you put it on –

MARION. No. Thank you. Truly.

NORMAN. Alright then. Have a nice evening.

MARION. Thank you. I'm sure I will.

(*MARION exits. BARBARA and GLENDA enter. This scene should be very stylized and quick.*)

NORMAN / BARBARA / GLENDA. (*Simultaneously:*) Hello. (*Slight chuckle.*)

NORMAN. You startled me.

GLENDA. I'm sorry.

BARBARA. Yes, very.

NORMAN. No matter. What can I do for you?

BARBARA. We need a room.

GLENDA. Yes, a double.

NORMAN. A double. I think we can handle that.

BARBARA. We?

NORMAN. Yes. My mother and myself. We don't get many guests this time of year, so we're grown accustomed to only a few.

GLENDA. Is that a problem?

NORMAN. No.

BARBARA. Alright.

NORMAN. Cash?

GLENDA. Yes.

BARBARA. Is that usual?

NORMAN. I'm sorry?

BARBARA. It's just that you said "cash" as if it were the usual way people paid in your establishment.

NORMAN. You just look like cash folks is all. Any bags.

GLENDA. No.

NORMAN. (*Writing in the ledger.*) No bags.

BARBARA. Why write that?

NORMAN. Legal purposes. You can't say something was stolen from your room if you don't have any bags.

BARBARA. Oh.

NORMAN. Which one of you ladies would like to sign in?

GLENDA. I will. T*takes the pen and signs the register without looking down.*)

NORMAN. "Glenda Johnson." I'll remember that. Aren't many Glenda's around anymore.

GLENDA. I'm sure.

NORMAN. Here's your key. Have a nice evening.

BARBARA. I'm sure we will.

(*BARBARA and GLENDA exit. NORMAN waits a moment, then exits.*

In MOTEL ROOM #1 MARION enters. She sets down her bag, then takes off her clothes down to a bra and slip. She pulls out an envelope stuffed with money, counts some of it, does some quick addition on a pad of paper, then tears up the page. She exits. We hear a shower running

In MOTEL ROOM #2 BARBARA and GLENDA enter.)

GLENDA. I'm exhausted. Let's go to sleep now and figure things out tomorrow.

BARBARA. I can't. Sleep, I mean. Because of what happened to Benni.

GLENDA. I believe that you believe what you told me about the burnt man in the hat, but you've got to sleep sometime. Now, if it will make you feel any better, we can sleep in shifts, and if anything strange happens, we'll wake the other person up. Okay?

BARBARA. Well, okay. I guess I should go first. Just so I can conquer this fear that I have.

GLENDA. That's the spirit! You lie down, and I'll wake you in four hours.

BARBARA. Alright.

(*BARBARA lies down and falls asleep. GLENDA tries to stay away, but falls asleep instantly.*

In MOTEL ROOM #1 – NORMAN, wearing a dress and wig, carrying a really big knife, enters. He looks around, then exits to the shower area. We hear screams and perhaps a familiar "Knifing a Blonde in the Shower" music.

In MOTEL ROOM #2 – GLENDA wakes up at the screams. He exits his room and crosses over to

MOTEL ROOM #1. GLENDA enters the room, exits to the shower area, then quickly reenters, aghast at the dead body in the shower he's just seen.)

GLENDA. (*Says the word:*) Gasp!

(*GLENDA exits MOTEL ROOM #1. NORMAN enters from shower area, then exits MOTEL ROOM #1.*)

GLENDA. (*Entering MOTEL ROOM #2.*) Barbara, wake up! I just saw a man in women's clothing!

BARBARA. (*Horrified and confused:*) What?!

GLENDA. He was murdering that girl in the next room. Come quick!

(*GLENDA and BARBARA exit.*

In the MOTEL LOBBY, NORMAN enters, sans women's clothes. He finishes up some work at the desk, then exits at some point before the end of the scene.

MOTEL ROOM #1. GLENDA and BARBARA race in.)

GLENDA. In there! I can't look!

BARBARA. (*Pokes her head into the shower area and recoils.*) Glen! (*GLENDA sad face.*) Da! (*GLENDA happy face.*) Do you know what this means?

GLENDA. Um, no.

BARBARA. The police are going to be looking for whoever murdered this girl. If they find us here, they'll think I did it! I already have a criminal record.

GLENDA. What should we do?

BARBARA. We have to get back on the road again. Until we straighten this whole mess out. Let's go!

(They exit out the door. SHIFT FOCUS TO—)

Scene Nine

(ROAD. BARBARA and GLENDA run in place for three steps then fall to the ground exhausted.)

GLENDA. I'm exhausted! I have to rest!

BARBARA. Just for a moment. Then we have to move on.

GLENDA. Where?

BARBARA. I see a light thru the woods over there.

GLENDA. That would be Camp Crystal Lake. I bet they don't have a telephone, or television, or radio, or newspaper or anything, so they won't know who we are. We could hide out –

(MILES races in, hysterical.)

MILES. You're next! You're next! They'll get you, too, and there's nothing you can do about it!

BARBARA. Sir, calm down! Who are you and what's the matter?

MILES. My name is Miles, and we have to get out of here before they get us, too!

GLENDA. What?

MILES. They're replacing people! One by one. In their sleep. I'm the only one left! They're after me and they'll be after you, too, when they find us!

BARBARA. See! I told you we shouldn't go to sleep.

MILES. Then you know!

BARBARA. Yes! When you go to sleep, the man in the hat comes to you in your dreams and if he kills you, you're really dead!

MILES. What? No! They're replacing people. They put these pod-like things beside you, and when you wake up you have no emotions, no feelings.

GLENDA. How can that be?

MILES. You've got to believe me! You're the only ones left!

GLENDA. What do we do? If we help him, we might get caught. But if what he says is true, it might be too late already.

BARBARA. Well –

(*A group of TOWNSPEOPLE burst in lead by THEODORA. They are emotionless, but quite threatening.*)

THEODORA. There he is. Grab them.

(*MILES runs away, chased by a group of TOWNSPEOPLE. Others grab GLENDA and BARBARA.*)

THEODORA. Take them back to town. We'll deal with them later.

(*A TOWNSPERSON returns.*)

THEODORA. Where is he?
TOWNSPERSON. He escaped.
THEODORA. No matter. We'll find him eventually. Back to town.
GLENDA. Who are you?
THEODORA. I am Theodora, if it matters.
GLENDA. No, who *are* you?
THEODORA. You'll find out soon enough. Take them back to town.

(*THEODORA and the TOWNSPEOPLE lead them in a circle back to where they were standing before. BARBARA and GLENDA are tied to chairs.*)

THEODORA. Here we are in town. If you were wise you wouldn't struggle. It will happen sooner or later. You must sleep sometime.
BARBARA. Why are you doing this?
THEODORA. For your own good. Once you've been replaced, you'll find yourself in a world with no pain, no emotions. Nothing to complicate your life in any way. Imagine a world with no wars, no hunger, no conflict.
BARBARA. And no love! You can't live without love! Sure, there are some bad parts about it. But without love, you're not living even if you are alive!
THEODORA. Once you've been replaced you will see our way is best.
GLENDA. You said no conflict, but even now you're forcing this upon us!
THEODORA. Those with knowledge are often seen as forcing it upon those untaught. You will see.

(*THEODORA and the TOWNSPEOPLE exit.*)

GLENDA. Oh, Barbara, I'm so tired.
BARBARA. Don't you dare! We'll get out of this somehow.
GLENDA. (*Falling asleep:*) But wouldn't it be nice to just close your eyes? It would all be over soon...

BARBARA. No!
GLENDA. Besides, we can't get out of these ropes...(*Sleeps.*)
BARBARA. Stop it!

(*MILES enters. He's been replaced.*)

BARBARA. Miles! (*Realizes:*) Oh, no! Not you!
MILES. They're right, Barbara. Just close your eyes and go to sleep.
BARBARA. They're not right! And damn you for giving up!

(*A TOWNSPERSON and KEVIN enter with pods [eggplants or gourds in the original production], which they place near BARBARA and GLENDA.*)
MILES. Look at your sister, Barbara. She knows. Just close your eyes.
BARBARA. Never!
MILES. You stand watch.
KEVIN. Yes.

(*MILES and TOWNSPERSON exit.*)

BARBARA. Get out of here!

(*KEVIN looks around, the frantically unties GLENDA and BARBARA.*)

BARBARA. What are you doing?
KEVIN. My name is Kevin. I'm not like them. And we've got to get out of here!
BARBARA. You're not like them? How come they haven't caught you yet?
KEVIN. You just have to show no emotion. That's how they spot you. Just walk around with a blank face and you can do whatever you want.
BARBARA. I'm not sure I believe you. This could be a trap.
KEVIN. You have to believe me. I'm your only chance.
BARBARA. Why? Why risk your life for us?
KEVIN. You sure ask a lot of questions. (*Indicates Glenda.*) Because of her. She's the most beautiful woman I've ever seen.
BARBARA. (*A beat.*) We need to have a talk.
KEVIN. Let's wake her up and get going. (*He shakes GLENDA.*)
GLENDA. (*Asleep:*) Just five more minutes...Just –

(*GLENDA opens his eyes to see KEVIN. A moment, deep gazes, hearts aflutter. MUSIC: Something romantic. Then as quickly as it started, MUSIC abruptly stops.*)

KEVIN. Okay, I'm going to open the door. We'll pretend it's already happened. Just don't show any emotions whatever you do, or they'll know. Here we go.

(*KEVIN, GLENDA and BARBARA move out to the STREET. The TOWNSPEOPLE mill about, emotionless. The trio starts to walk. BARTOWSKI, now "replaced," passes.*)

BARBARA. Barfowski!

(*All the TOWNSPEOPLE stop and stare at them.*)

BARBARA. (*Realizes:*) Oh...right...
KEVIN. Run!

(*KEVIN, GLENDA and BARBARA run in place downstage as the TOWNSPEOPLE give chase by running in place upstage. Gradually the TOWNSPEOPLE fade offstage as KEVIN, GLENDA and BARBARA outrun them. Once the crowd leaves -)*

KEVIN. You two go that way, and I'll lead them over there to mislead them.
GLENDA. You can't! They'll catch you!
KEVIN. No, they won't! One person can run faster than three. You go and I'll find you later.
BARBARA. Where?
KEVIN. Camp Crystal Lake. I know they haven't been there yet. I don't think they even know it exists.
GLENDA. Promise me you'll come back!
BARBARA. They're coming! I can hear them!
GLENDA. Promise!
KEVIN. I promise! Now get going! Hey! I'm over here you zombie sons-a-bitches! (*He exits.*)
BARBARA. Come on. He'll be alright.
GLENDA. (*Wistfully:*) I'll never forget him.

(*GLENDA and BARBARA exit. SHIFT FOCUS TO—*)

Scene Ten

(*CABIN, Camp Crystal Lake, 1980's. BRIAN, MICHAEL, CHUCK, MICHELE, DIANE and MARIANNE, all camp counselors, enter smoking pot and drinking.*)

BRIAN. (*Pot voice:*) Great shit.
MICHELE. (*Pot voice:*) Where'd ya get it?
MICHAEL. From that weird couple across the lake, Jack and Mae. They always have the best stuff, and they hardly ever charge me for it.
CHUCK. Cool!

DIANE. Way cool!

MARIANNE. Way-er cool. (*Everyone falls into hysterical pot laughter.*)

BRIAN. (*Laughing:*) That's so not funny!

DIANE. (*Laughing:*) I know! I hate her! (*More laughter all around.*)

BRIAN. I have a cool idea. Let's play Monopoly!

DIANE. Way to live on the edge, Brian.

MICHAEL. Yeah, I can barely contain myself.

BRIAN. No, stupids. Not just Monopoly. Strip Monopoly.

MARIANNE. What?

BRIAN. Strip Monopoly! Instead of rent, you pay in clothes.

MICHELE. I'm in!

CHUCK. I don't know...

MICHELE. Chicken?

BRIAN. No, he just has a tiny wang. (*Everyone laughs.*)

CHUCK. Shut up! I'm in!

MARIANNE. (*Nervously:*) I'm in. I guess.

MICHELE. Yes! (*She high-five's Marianne.*)

BRIAN. Diane? Mike?

MICHAEL. I don't think so.

DIANE. And it's not because he has a tiny wang.

BRIAN. So he has a big wang?

DIANE. Yes...I mean, no...shut up!

MICHAEL. It's just that we have better places to get naked than in front of you losers.

ALL. Ooooohhh....

MICHAEL. And with that, we shall depart.

DIANE. Bye.

(*DIANE and MICHAEL exit.*)

BRIAN. (*Calling off:*) Later! Have a nice fuck! I mean, good night!

DIANE. (*Off:*) It's called making love!

MICHELE. I'm the hat.

MARIANNE. I'm the shoe.

CHUCK. You are not the hat. I'm always the hat.

MICHELE. You are not always the hat. This is the first time we've played together.

CHUCK. I mean, in the grand scheme of things, I'm always the hat.

MARIANNE. Well, you know what Freud said about hats? (*She holds up her fingers to indicate something very small.*)

MICHELE. Marianne!

BRIAN. (*Laughing:*) I'm shocked and appalled!

CHUCK. Shut up! Then I'll be the dog. (*All burst out laughing.*) What?

BRIAN. Nothing, nothing. Swear. Let's just play.

(They set up the game. SHIFT FOCUS TO —)

Scene Eleven

(FOREST. DIANE and MICHAEL are making out.)

DIANE. What was that?
MICHAEL. My hand, I swear!
DIANE. No, that noise.
MICHAEL. What noise?
DIANE. That crunching footsteps noise.
MICHAEL. Somebody's walking on Cracklin' Oat Bran. Come on, Diane.
DIANE. Brian, if that's you, you're a dead man!
MICHAEL. Diane, nobody's out there. Relax.
DIANE. I heard something snap!
MICHAEL. It's my heart breaking, honey, because you keep stopping me. No one followed us from the house. They're all too stoned.
DIANE. Well, okay. If you say so.

(They go back to making out. MUSIC: Perhaps the familiar "Teenagers Getting Murdered In the Woods After Having Sex" music. A SHAPE steps out of the darkness, carrying a huge knife and perhaps wearing a hockey mask. He grabs MICHAEL by the hair and cuts his throat, splattering blood on Diane. Much screaming until the finished off DIANE as well. The SHAPE exits. DIANA and MICHAEL's bodies remain on the ground. SHIFT FOCUS TO —)

Scene Twelve

(CABIN. The Monopoly game continues.)

MARIANNE. *(Reacting to the screams:)* What was that?
CHUCK. Thunder.
MARIANNE. It sounded like a scream to me.

(GLENDA and BARBARA burst in.)

MICHELE. What the fuck?
BARBARA. Thank goodness!
CHUCK. Who are you people?
GLENDA. You've got to help us! There's a bunch of people after us, and you, too, if they find us!
BRIAN. What?
BARBARA. Everybody in that town has gone crazy! There's zombies, and murder, and giants and pods that replace people and prison that is bad, nightmare killer people –

CHUCK. Get her some more dope. She's nuts.

GLENDA. She's not nuts! It's true. And your lives are in as much danger as ours are!

MARIANNE. Okay, calm down. Let's just take this from the beginning. Everybody just sit down. Now, start from the top.

GLENDA. (*Big sigh:*) Okay, first –

(*MUSIC UP. GLENDA and BARBARA pantomime their entire adventure to this point as the SHAPE crosses thru the forest. Immediately after the SHAPE exits MUSIC OUT.*)

GLENDA. – and then we came here.

MARIANNE. Wow.

MICHELE. No way.

BRIAN. In any case, we better find Diane and Michael. I'll be right back.

MARIANNE. You can't go alone!

CHUCK. I'll go with you.

BRIAN. No, stay here. Somebody has to look after the girls.

GLENDA / BARBARA / MICHELE / MARIANNE. Hey!

BRIAN. Sorry. Besides, I'll be fine. I'll take a flashlight.

(*Everyone is reassured. BRIAN exits.*)

MARIANNE. Let's get you out of those wet clothes.

CHUCK. (*Leering at Glenda:*) Yeah, let's.

MARIANNE. Stop it. Come on. I've got some things you can wear. You both look about my size.

(*MARIANNE leads GLENDA and BARBARA off.*)

MICHELE. Do you believe them?

CHUCK. No way. But let Brian find those guys and we can all chill out here for awhile. At least until morning.

(*MICHELE and CHUCK put the Monopoly game away. SHIFT FOCUS TO —*)

Scene Thirteen

(*FOREST. BRIAN is searching with his flashlight.*)

BRIAN. Mike? Diane? You're not going to believe what just happened at the cabin. These two chicks just showed up! One of them's kinda ugly looking. But her mom is hot! (*Is startled by someone offstage.*) Oh! Shit! You scared me! What are you doing out here? It's raining –

(*BRIAN moves close to the exit. He reacts as if he's being stabbed, then falls backwards onto the stage, covered in blood. His body remains onstage. SHIFT FOCUS TO –*)

Scene Fourteen

(*CABIN. MARIANNE, GLENDA and BARBARA enter. GLENDA and BARBARA have changed into some of MARIANNE's clothes.*)

MARIANNE. Where are those guys? It's been over an hour. Maybe we should go look for them.

BARBARA. We've got to go in a group. They'll pick us off one by one if we go alone.

CHUCK. How about you guys stay here and Michele and I will go look for them. That way there'll be two groups and nobody alone.

GLENDA. I don't know. There's an awful lot of them.

MICHELE. We'll be fine. Come on, Chuck.

MARIANNE. Five minutes, then we come looking for you.

MICHELE. Is five minutes long enough?

CHUCK. I think we'll need an hour, but we'll take what we can get. (*They crack up and exit.*)

MARIANNE. Those two. They make me so mad, making fun of us like that.

BARBARA. At least they're out looking.

MARIANNE. Yeah, down each others' pants.

GLENDA. Five minutes. Oh, where's Kevin?

MARIANNE. Who?

GLENDA. (*Haughtily:*) A friend.

MARIANNE. Oh.

(*They wait. SHIFT FOCUS TO –*)

Scene Fifteen

(*FOREST. MICHELE and CHUCK enter and sit.*)

CHUCK. Okay, here we are. I've got a big surprise for you.

MICHELE. *You've* got a big surprise?

CHUCK. Yeah. Close your eyes?

MICHELE. (*Closes her eyes.*) Okay.

CHUCK. You're peeking!

MICHELE. I'm not!

(They argue the peeking issue. The SHAPE enters with a drill connected to a very long extension cord. He drills CHUCK and MICHELE to death, then exits. CHUCK and MICHELE's bodies stay onstage. SHIFT FOCUS TO –)

Scene Sixteen

(CABIN.)

GLENDA. That's five. Oh, where's Kevin?
MARIANNE. Okay, let's go. I'll go get my coat and a flashlight. You wait here.
BARBARA. Hurry!
(MARIANNE exits. BARBARA and GLENDA wait...and wait...and wait. Finally-)

GLENDA. Where do you supposed she keeps her coat?

(Bang! Bang! Bang! A loud knock on the door startles them.)

GLENDA. Kevin!

(GLENDA yanks open the door. MRS. VOORHEES enters.)

BARBARA. Oh! You startled us!
MRS. VOORHEES. I'm so sorry. I'm sure I didn't mean to.
GLENDA. Who are you?
MRS. VOORHEES. Why, I'm Mrs. Voorhees. I live down the way. I used to work at this camp. My son, Jason, spent several summers here.
BARBARA. Mrs. Voorhees, do you have a car? We need to get out of here. Something weird is going on in this town, and we need to get help.
MRS. VOORHEES. Weird? As in?
BARBARA. Well, most recently all of the counselors here at the camp have disappeared, including Marianne, who just went in there for her coat.
MRS. VOORHEES. What? Now, that's just nonsense. Let me look.

(MRS. VOORHEES opens the door to MARIANNE's room. MARIANNE's body falls to the ground.)

BARBARA / GLENDA. *(Scream:)* AAAAAAHHHHHH!!
MRS. VOORHEES. Oh, my goodness! It's happening again! I told them not to reopen this camp. Do you know what the people of the town call this camp? Camp Blood. That's because a little boy died here at Camp Crystal Lake. Drowned. In the lake. While the counselors who were

supposed to be watching him were off having sex. SEX! While they were supposed to be watching him. And that's when the killings began. They closed this camp down for fifteen years. Until this summer. I knew they shouldn't have tried. And all because of what happened to that little boy. That beautiful, little boy. Jason was his name. So young. (*Jason's voice:*) Help me! Help me, Mommy! (*Normal:*) I'm coming Jason! You see. I had to stop them. I couldn't let this camp open again. Not after what they did to my Jason! (*Jason's voice:*) Kill them! Kill them, Mommy! (*Normal:*) I am Jason!

(*MRS. VOORHEES pulls out a huge knife. GLENDA and BARBARA scream and run. SHIFT FOCUS TO –*)

Scene Seventeen

(*FOREST. Chase scene thru the forest. MRS. VOORHEES chases GLENDA and BARBARA thru the forest. As they pass each dead counselor the bodies come back to life as zombies, struggle to their feet and join the chase. GLENDA and BARBARA make a full circle and end up back in the cabin.*

SHIFT FOCUS TO – CABIN. GLENDA and BARBARA race in and shut the door. MRS. VOORHEES bursts in.)

MRS. VOORHEES. It's useless! You can't hide. Because I've got so much help!

(*NORMAN enters, wearing a dress and wig, carrying a knife.*)

NORMAN. (*Mother's voice:*) Kill them, Norman.
MRS. VOORHEES. (*Jason's voice:*) I am, Mommy.

(*THEODORA enters.*)

THEODORA. You just have to go to sleep.

(*BURNT MANIAC enters.*)

BURNT MANIAC. Yes, sleep...

(*BARTOWSKI enters.*)

BARTOWSKI. You're gonna spend a lot of time in the hole...

(*More zombies and pod people enter. SPLIT FOCUS BETWEEN CABIN AND OUTSIDE CABIN. ALLISON enters, menacing a miniature version of the cabin. BARBARA and GLENDA see her past the fourth wall.*)

ALLISON. HARRY?! WHERE'S HARRY?!
MRS. VOORHEES. So you see, it's no use fighting. We will get you. One way or another.

(*KEVIN enters outside the cabin. He ties a rope across the path of ALLISON, i.e. across the stage. He shouts up to her.*)

KEVIN. Hey! I'm over here, you fifty foot bitch!
ALLISON. HARRY?! (*She turns toward the cabin.*)
GLENDA. Kevin?!
KEVIN. (*Appears in the doorway of the cabin.*) Come on! Run!

(*GLENDA and BARBARA fight their way past their foes in the cabin and follow KEVIN out. They slam the door behind them, trapping everyone inside.*

IN SPLIT SCREEN - ALLISON gets her foot tangled in the rope, trips, and falls onto the cabin. Everyone inside the cabin screams as they are crushed to death. BLACKOUT.)

Epilogue

(*LIGHTS UP. KEVIN, GLENDA and BARBARA enter.*)

BARBARA. That was horrible. All of them crushed to death.
GLENDA. But it's over now. Right, Kevin?
KEVIN. Yes, Glenda. It's all over.

(*GLENDA takes KEVIN's arm, and the trio happily exit. MUSIC: Perhaps "Dead People Get Back Up At the End" music. All the crushed zombies, etc., slowly rise up and head toward the audience. BLACKOUT.*)

THE END?

Bitches

A comedy in two acts by

Sean Abley

Bitches, original program art, Factory Theater, Chicago IL, 1999

Copyright Protection. This play (the "Play") is fully protected under the copyright laws of the United States of America and all countries with which the United States has reciprocal copyright relations, whether through bilateral or multilateral treaties or otherwise, and including, but not limited to, all countries covered by the Pan-American Copyright Convention, the Universal Copyright Convention, and the Berne Convention.

Reservation of Rights. All rights to this Play are strictly reserved, including, without limitation, professional and amateur stage performance rights; motion picture, recitation, lecturing, public reading, radio broadcasting, television, video, and sound recording rights; rights to all other forms of mechanical or electronic reproduction now known or yet to be invented, such as CD-ROM, CD-I, DVD, photocopying, and information storage and retrieval systems; and the rights of translation into non-English languages.

Performance Licensing and Royalty Payments. Amateur, stock and professional performance rights to this Play are controlled exclusively by Plays To Order ("PTO"). No amateur or stock production groups or individuals may perform this Play without obtaining advance written permission. Required royalty fees for performing this play are available from PTO. Such royalty fees may be subject to change without notice. Although this book may have been obtained for a particular licensed performance, such performance rights, if any, are not transferable. Required royalties must be paid every time the Play is performed before any audience, whether or not it is presented for profit and whether or not admission is charged. All licensing requests and inquiries concerning amateur, stock and professional performance rights should be addressed to PTO at sean@playstoorder.com or Sean Abley, 5724 Hollywood Blvd. Suite 109, Los Angeles CA 90028

Restriction of Alterations. There shall be no deletions, alterations, or changes of any kind made to the Play, including changing the gender, the cutting of dialogue, or alteration of objectionable language, unless directly authorized by playwright. The title of the Play shall not be altered.

Author Credit. Any individual or group receiving permission to produce this Play is required to give credit to the author as the sole and exclusive author of the Play. This obligation applies to the title page of every program distributed in connection with performances of the play, and in any instance that the title of the Play appears for purposes of advertising, publicizing, or otherwise exploiting the Play and or/production thereof. The name of the author must appear on a separate line, in which no other name appears, immediately beneath the title and of a font size at least 50% as large as the largest letter used in the title of the Play. No person, firm, or entity may receive credit larger or more prominent that that accorded the author. The name of the author may not be abbreviated or otherwise altered from the form in which it appears in this Play.

Publisher Attribution. All programs, advertisements, and other printed material distributed or published in connection with the amateur, stock or professional production of the Play shall include the following notice:

Produced by special arrangement with Plays To Order.
(www.PlaysToOrder.com)

Bitches, Factory Theater, Chicago 1993.
Clockwise from top left: Kirk Pynchon, Sean Abley, Joey Meyer, Michael Hayes

ACKNOWLEDGEMENTS

Bitches was first presented by Some Mo' Productions in association with the Factory Theater, Chicago, Illinois, on September 3, 1993. The production was directed by Sean Abley and Amy Seeley, stage managed by Amy Seeley. Choreography by Kirk Pynchon. Suzy B's Uniforms designed by Carl Andruskevich. Makeup and wig design by Amy Seeley. "Pontificate with Paula" theme written by Dave Springer and Sheldon Wheaton. The cast was as follows:

ANGELATINA VINDECHI.........................	Kirk Pynchon
SINDEE SANDSTONE.............................	Sean Abley
CARMELLE CONSTANTINE.....................	Joey Meyer
PEPPER SALTIMBEAUX...........................	Michael Hayes
LILA DENCH...	Carl Andruskevich
KATHY GRAHAM..................................	Jesse Dienstag
RUBY..	Mike Beyer
VERA VINDECHI...................................	Jim Blanchette
CHARLENE SANDSTONE.........................	Mike Meredith
PAULA DEMARCATO.............................	Scott Parkinson
TERRI...	Bo Blackburn
GRETCHEN, BENNI, COP #2, REPORTER, FOREPERSON, WOMEN ASSASSINS........	George Brant
JANET / COP #1 / JUDGE...........................	Brian Sheridan

The Los Angeles premiere of *Bitches* was presented by The Magnum Players on October 3, 2014. The production was directed by Sean Abley; produced by Brandon Clark; and stage-managed by Aaron Francis. Production design by Brandon Clark. Sound design by Jaime Robledo. Talk show themes by Michael Teoli. Publicity by Philip Sokoloff. Photography by Anousha Hutton. Logo design by Mike Ross. Poster design Marty Yu. The cast was as follows:

ANGELATINA VINDECHI.......................	Matt Valle
SINDEE SANDSTONE.............................	Drew Droege
CARMELLE...	Michael Vaccaro
PEPPER...	Timothy Joshua Hearl
LILA DENCH...	James Jaeger
KATHY GRAHAM, JANET, CHEERLEADER HOPEFUL...............	Brad Griffith
RUBY, CHEERLEADER HOPEFUL, LADY ASSASSIN.....................................	Sean Abley
VERA VINDECHI...................................	Jim Blanchette
CHARLENE SANDSTONE.........................	Sam Pancake
PAULA DEMARCATO.............................	Ralph Cole, Jr.
TERRI...	Thomas Colby
ALL THE OTHER WOMEN.......................	Jason Looney
UNDERSTUDY......................................	Esteban Cruz

CHARACTERS

SINDEE SANDSTONE — Evil teen, leader of the pack.
ANGELATINA VINDECHI — Nice teen, new girl in town.
CARMELLE — Friend of Sindee, easily manipulated.
PEPPER — Friend of Sindee, a little meaner and a little dumber than Carmelle.
CHARLENE SANDSTONE — Sindee's mom, domineering, a terrible person.
VERA VINDECHI — Angelatina's mom, the best mom ever.
KATHY GRAHAM — Charlene's friend, easily manipulated.
RUBY — Hard-bitten waitress, Charlene's friend, crass.
MS. DENCH — Gym teacher and cheerleading coach.
PAULA DEMARCATO — Talk show hostess. The Devil.
TERRI — Her assistant… grudgingly.
HOUSEWIFE – Abused spouse.
JANET — Talk show guest with problems.
GRETCHEN – Same.
BENNI — Tough prison inmate.
WOMAN — Assassin, but can you blame her?
WOMAN #2 – Ditto
NURSE
POLICEWOMAN
REPORTER
FEMALE JUDGE
LADY FOREWOMAN
LADY WARDEN (VOICE)
OTHER CHEERLEADERS HOPEFULS

NOTE: This character list reflects the Los Angeles production, which reworked the script to make the "All the other women" a quick-change role. Also, I prefer the cast of *Bitches* to be all male. There's never been an all-female production of *Bitches*, so I can't really provide any pros or cons to that approach. So if you want to give that a shot, have at it. But having a mixed cast, men and women, would be a no-no.

SETTING

Tubbville, IL, USA

TIME

Probably sometime in the 90s.

TO DRAG OR NOT TO DRAG AND OTHER COSTUME NOTES

The original production of *Bitches* was in full drag, as were all the subsequent productions until the Los Angeles version. For some reason I decided to stage the L.A. production in men's clothing (okay, truth, I didn't want to shave my beard), and I have to say, it worked really well, and certainly framed the socio-political statement I was trying to make in a different way.

There comes a point in the play at the top of Act Two where the actor playing "All the other women" is changing character from line to line. In the LA production we totally copped to the fact it was one actor, and had him dress in a basic black outfit, then had him changes small pieces, sometimes on stage, to represent each character.

TO DANCE OR NOT TO DANCE

The original production opened on a complicated cheerleading dance tryout. I've left this in the script, but don't let it deter you from producing the play if you don't have dancers. The Los Angeles production cut the routine, opening instead with a cheer in the dark, then lights up on the girls bouncing around as if they'd just finished their tryout.

THE GARDENS

In several productions most of the scene changes were accomplished by painting four theatrical blocks different colors on each side, with one side including plastic flowers as a "garden." One color was the school, one color was Paula's set, etc. The actors would rotate the blocks as they entered as if it were part of the business of the scene.

Bitches, The Magnum Players, Los Angeles 2014.
Left to right: Matt Valle, Timothy Joshua Hearl, Michael Vaccaro, Drew Droege

BITCHES

By Sean Abley

ACT ONE

Scene One

(*SUSAN B. ANTHONY HIGH SCHOOL GYMNASIUM. On the stage as the audience files in is a sign on a chair:*

> Susan B. Anthony High School
> CHEERLEADER TRYOUTS!!!
> Final Cuts Today!

LIGHTS go to BLACK. We hear MUSIC. Something hip-hop with a great beat. LIGHTS FADE UP. Cheerleading tryouts. SINDEE, PEPPER, CARMELLE, ANGELATINA and the other CHEERLEADER HOPEFULS do a complicated, funky cheerleading routine.[NOTE: This on-stage tryout can be cut as per production notes.] After they finish, MS. DENCH, gym teacher and cheerleading coach, enters.)

DENCH. Alright, ladies, that was very nice. Very nice indeedy. Susan B. Anthony High School would be proud to have any of you on the squad. Unfortunately, there are only three spots on the Suzy Bees, so four of you are going to have to go home disappointed. I know it's an emotional time, and I'll try to comfort you the best I know how.
SINDEE. I bet.
DENCH. Don't start with me, Sindee! Your lip is what's going to keep you off the Suzy Bees.
SINDEE. That's just 'cause you want to use my lips for something else.
DENCH. (*Furious:*) Take a lap!
SINDEE. Why don't you make me?
DENCH. Look, Sandstone! I don't care if your mother is the social chair of the Tubbville Ladies Auxiliary. You better get your ass around that track before I kick it around!

(*It's a standoff. Finally SINDEE exits for a lap.*)

DENCH. It's just as well she's gone. I've got the results of the tryout right here. Read 'em and weep.

(*Dench posts the list and exits. The girls excitedly push one CHEERLEADER HOPEFUL toward the list. She checks, doesn't find her name, runs off crying.*)

CHEERLEADER HOPEFUL. (*Crying:*) Why??? Why??? (*Exits.*)

(*The group pushes the second CHEERLEADER HOPEFUL forward. She checks the list, doesn't find herself on it, races off crying as she tries to cut herself with a ballpoint pen.*)

CHEERLEADER HOPEFUL. (*Crying:*) I cut myself so I can feel!!!! (*Exits.*)

(*The girls push the third CHEERLEADER HOPEFUL toward the list. She checks, doesn't find herself, and makes a comically extended exit, crying all the way. PEPPER and CARMELLE shove their way to the list.*)

PEPPER. Move it, Angelatina!
CARMELLE. Yeah, blow.

(*They push ANGELATINA out of the way. They scream in excitement as they realize they made it. Then* —)

PEPPER. Holy shit.
ANGELATINA. What?
CARMELLE. Sindee's gonna shit a brick!
ANGELATINA. What? What? (*She pushes her way to the list.*) Oh my goodness! Oh my goodness! I made it! I'm a Suzy Bee!

(*SINDEE enters, panting.*)

ANGELATINA. Isn't it great!
SINDEE. Isn't what great?
ANGELATINA. I made it! I'm a Suzy Bee!
SINDEE. What?
CARMELLE. It's true.
SINDEE. You're kidding.
ANGELATINA. Isn't it exciting?
SINDEE. I'm thrilled. So, which one of you sorry sluts didn't make the squad?
PEPPER. Well…
SINDEE. Move it. (*Reads list:*) Alternate?
CARMELLE. Now, Sindee…
SINDEE. Alternate?!
PEPPER. Now, Sindee, it's not that bad -
SINDEE. That fucking BITCH MADE ME AN ALTERNATE!! THAT STUPID LESBO MARTINA NAVRATILOVA WANNA-BE MADE ME AN ALTERNATE!!!
CARMELLE. Now Sindee, maybe a spot will open up. Maybe somebody will get hurt. And there's always next year.

SINDEE. There is no next year, stupid! I'm a senior! This was my last chance. I'm supposed to be captain of this fucking squad!

ANGELATINA. You're a senior? Wow. I'm only a sophomore.

(They all stare at her.)

ANGELATINA. Gosh. Well, I'll see you gals at practice. *(She holds out her hand to shake. The other girls don't move.)* Congratulations, Pepper. Congratulations, Carmelle. No hard feelings, huh Sindee?

SINDEE. *(Clearing her throat as if to spit on ANGELATINA's hand.)*

ANGELATINA. Well. Anyway. See you at practice! *(She exits.)*

CARMELLE. What are we gonna do?

SINDEE. Quit whining, Carmelle.

PEPPER. Yeah, quit whining.

SINDEE. Shut up.

CARMELLE. Well, I'm sorry, but it won't be the same. You have to be on the team. We planned it that way. There must be something we can do. Let's see. The only way an alternate—

SINDEE. Stop saying that word! Pepper, gimme a cig.

PEPPER. Here.

CARMELLE. The only was an... um... substitute can be on the squad is if one of the regular members can't make it. Like if they're sick or something.

SINDEE. So which one of you is gonna get sick?

PEPPER. Sindee!

CARMELLE. No way!

SINDEE. Alright, alright! Don't get your undies in a bunch. It's that Vindechi bitch we gotta get rid of.

CARMELLE. How?

SINDEE. Well, it can't be me. I gotta be as far away as possible when it happens, 'cause I'm the prime suspect.

PEPPER. We still don't know how.

SINDEE. Don't worry about that. I'll figure it out. Come on. I need something chocolate.

PEPPER / CARMELLE. Me too!

(They start to exit. DENCH enters.)

DENCH. Well, well. It looks like we got two thirds of our Suzy Bees here. And Sindee, too.

SINDEE. I'll get you for this, Dench! My mother —

DENCH. — is the social chairman of the Kiss My Ass Society of Tubbville. Turn that record over, Sandstone. I've heard that side already. As long as it's my gym and my cheerleading squad you play by my rules. Got it?

SINDEE. Shove it.

DENCH. Oh, I will. Down your throat. You know, you little rich bitches make me sick, and the only thing that makes me feel better is dumping you on your ass. And I feel real good right now. Now get out of my gym.

SINDEE. (*Under her breath:*) ...Dyke...

DENCH. What?

SINDEE. I'm so sorry. That was rude of me. What I mean to say was...DYKE!

(*The three girls squeal with laughter and race out. SHIFT FOCUS TO—*)

Scene Two

(*SANDSTONE HOME. Meeting of the Ladies Auxiliary. MRS. SANDSTONE [with a martini], MRS. VINDECHI [lady drink with umbrella], MRS. GRAHAM [scotch on the rocks], and RUBY [beer] are in attendance. We sense they may be a little drunk.*)

KATHY. ...and they were swapping husbands! Can you believe it?

RUBY. Swapping them for what? A new toaster?

(*They all laugh.*)

VERA. (*Covering her mouth:*) Oh, stop! I can't believe I'm laughing at that. It's so bad... hee hee hee...

CHARLENE. Oh, loosen up, Vera. Let your girdle out a notch.

(*They laugh.*)

VERA. I do not wear a girdle!

KATHY. Oh, come on. If you hit somethin' sharp, you'd fly outta that thing like Pillsbury cookie dough.

(*More laughter.*)

RUBY. (*During the laughter.*) She is hugely fat...

VERA. I think some of the ladies at the meeting today have had a little too much loosey juicy. And I think that's causing the language to get a little... rough.

CHARLENE. You mean bitchy? If you don't like it, why don't you leave? Remember, Mrs. Vera Vindechi, you shouldn't even be at a Tubbville Ladies Auxiliary meeting. You haven't lived here for over a year. So, unless you want to go back to drinking cooking sherry and watching "Wife Swap" marathons alone each afternoon, I suggest you catch up with the program.

VERA. (*Silence, then haughtily:*) I have to use the powder room. Excuse me.

RUBY. (*To KATHY*) Why? Did ya fart?

(*They laugh. VERA flounces out.*)

RUBY. (*In the laughter:*) I really do think there was an odor...

CHARLENE. That tight-ass really puts a cramp in my style.

RUBY. God put a cramp in your style.

CHARLENE. Ruby, don't you have to get back to the diner?

RUBY. My shift doesn't start for another half hour. You're not gonna get rid of me that easy.

KATHY. Separate corners, girls, separate corners. Let's at least talk some business before "Oprah" comes on.

(*VERA enters.*)

CHARLENE. We'd better wait until her highness gets back or she'll throw a snit.

VERA. Present and accounted for, sans snit.

KATHY. Okay, last year you weren't around, Vera, but we started a thing where we have a contest throughout the community and all the entrance fees go to a good cause. Oh, what was it last year...?

RUBY. Starving kids or something.

CHARLENE. I think it was crack.

VERA. There's crack in Tubbville?

RUBY. Only in the back of my plumber's pants.

(*They laugh.*)

RUBY. I'm the funny one!

VERA. (*From behind her hand:*) Hee... hee... hee... Stop it!

KATHY. That's it. It was crack babies. Just horrible. So we had all the money go to...oh, what was it called? "Operation Safe Distance," that was it. So the mothers, the horrible, drug-addicted, homeless mothers who did this to their babies in the first place would never see their children again.

VERA. Hooray!

RUBY. Last year we had an origami contest. Sin Lu from Bamboo Heaven, over in the mall? She was the judge.

VERA. Oh, Sin Lu! I met her last week. She is so sweet. Is she a member of the Auxiliary?

CHARLENE. Of course not!

(*Awkward silence while the others stare at VERA.*)

KATHY. Anyway, we need to come up with something new for this year's contest.

RUBY. How about a hot dog eating contest? The diner could supply the wieners.

KATHY. Mmmm, no. But my husband would sure like to watch me practice.

(*They laugh.*)

RUBY. That's called fe-latch-io! It's French!

VERA. (*From behind her hand:*) Hee hee hee... Stop it!

KATHY. How about a dance-a-thon?

CHARLENE. And ruin my hair? I don't think so. Besides, I'm a Baptist.

VERA. How about a beautiful garden contest?

CHARLENE. I know! How about a beautiful garden contest?

KATHY / RUBY. Perfect! Lovely! etc.

CHARLENE. We'll call it "How Green Is My Valley" and everyone will have two months to get her garden together.

ALL. Hooray! etc.

KATHY. I'll get the flyers printed and all that, and we'll meet next week to get started.

VERA. I'm so excited!

KATHY. So, unless there's some other business, we'll adjourn the meeting.

RUBY. I'll second that.

KATHY. Meeting adjourned. Ruby, do you want a lift to the diner?

RUBY. (*Chugging her beer.*) Sure, hon. Thanks.

KATHY. Bye, Charlene! Thanks for the use of your rec room.

(*KATHY and RUBY exit. SINDEE storms in, bumping into VERA.*)

VERA. Oh, excuse me Sindee! Say, have you seen Angelatina?

SINDEE. Yeah. (*A beat, then she storms out.*)

VERA. (*Awkward silence*) Oh... well, thanks. Bye Charlene. (*She exits.*)

CHARLENE. Bye! (*Under her breath:*) Don't let the door hit your ass...

(*SINDEE re-enters with a bag of potato chips, eating them furiously.*)

CHARLENE. Sindee, what are you doing? Sindee, stop! Stop it! Sindee! Snap, little miss! (*She grabs the bag away.*) Now darling, what's the matter?

SINDEE. Nothing! Leave me alone!

CHARLENE. Sindee Sandstone, you only binge when something is wrong, so you better fess up, Miss Ma'am.

SINDEE. I didn't make the cheerleading squad.

(CHARLENE slaps her.)

CHARLENE. Don't you ever talk like that while I'm alive! What do you mean, you didn't make the cheerleading squad?

SINDEE. Angelatina took my spot, and she's only a sophomore! I hate that little bitch!

CHARLENE. Well, obviously you weren't trying hard enough. You're grounded.

SINDEE. What?!

CHARLENE. You and I and everyone else knows you should be on that squad. How are you going to be Queen of the Spring Formal if you're not captain of the cheerleading squad? I was Queen of the Spring Formal, as was your grandmother, and I will not have you breaking that royal lineage. So until you figure out how to regain the position that is rightfully yours, you're grounded. No losers in my family. *(Hands her back the bag of chips.)* And when you're done with these, go make yourself throw up, because it's almost time for dinner. *(Moves toward the exit.)*

SINDEE. Kitchen's that way, Mom…

CHARLENE. Kitchen's where mommy says it is! Let's go!

(SINDEE and CHARLENE exit. SHIFT FOCUS TO –)

Scene Three

(TV STUDIO / SUBURBAN HOME. The "Pontificate with Paula" show is taping. The THEME MUSIC plays. PAULA is a brash talk show host, 30s. She is in the studio berating a HOUSEWIFE who has called in to the show from her home.)

PAULA. Okay, we're back, so let's take another caller. Hello, pontificate with Paula.

HOUSEWIFE. *(On phone:)* Hello? Hello? Uh, hello -

PAULA. Oh, let's not play that "Hello, hello, am I on?" game, shall we? Speak up!

HOUSEWIFE. *(On phone:)* Well, I can identify with the topic because I'm being abused by my husband.

PAULA. So?

HOUSEWIFE. *(On phone:)* Uh… well… don't you want to talk about it? I thought that's why you took calls.

PAULA. Oh, well, alright. When did he hit you last?

HOUSEWIFE. *(On phone:)* Last night. He came home late and I'd already made dinner with the kids. He was mad we hadn't waited.

PAULA. And?

HOUSEWIFE. *(On phone:)* What?

PAULA. And? Get on with it.

HOUSEWIFE. (*On phone:*) Well...

PAULA. You didn't wait, and I'm supposed to crucify this guy on national television because his temper flared up a little?

HOUSEWIFE. (*On phone, incredulous:*) What?

PAULA. Look, honey. You know what the problem is, so solve it, for cripes sake. You just spelled it out for me right here. Stop wasting your husband's and my time and get on the ball.

HOUSEWIFE. (*On phone:*) You're insane!

PAULA. Yeah, and you know what? I've got my own TV show. (*She hangs up the phone.*) Let's take a question from the audience. You, over there.

(*A WOMAN stands up in the audience.*)

WOMAN. I've got a question.

PAULA. Yes?

WOMAN. Which do you prefer, Smith or Wesson?

(*She draws a gun and points it at PAULA. Commotion. TERRI, Paula's assistant, rushes on.*)

PAULA. Terri, do something!

WOMAN. You're the devil!

PAULA. Terri!

WOMAN. Don't take one more step, or I'll blow her guts out!

(*TERRI very purposefully takes a deliberate step forward. The WOMAN shoots and hits PAULA in the arm.*)

PAULA. I'm shot!

TERRI. Damn! (*As in, "she missed!"*)

PAULA. Grab her, you idiot!

(*TERRI wrestles the WOMAN for the gun, yanking it out of her hand. PAULA grabs the gun from TERRI and points it at the WOMAN.*)

PAULA. Move away from her. Who are you?

WOMAN. I represent women -

(*PAULA shoots her in the throat. The WOMAN falls offstage.*)

PAULA. That's it for today. Join me tomorrow on "Pontificate With Paula." (*Holds as the theme music plays. Cameras off.*) Terri, my lovely assistant. Where the fuck were you? Gail would have taken that bullet for Oprah.

TERRI. She gets paid a little bit more than minimum wage.

PAULA. Your father owns this pathetic production company, so don't pull that with me you little bitch! We both know this "assistant" bullshit is because he made me take you on so you'd know the ropes for when he croaks and leaves it all to you.

TERRI. I'd guess that would mean you should be a little nicer to me then, huh?

PAULA. Don't count on it. By the time that geezer kicks I'll have my own production company, and then TransWorld can kiss my crack. You first.

TERRI. Can't wait. Meantime, you have promos to tape at 4:30. You should stop by wardrobe and see if they can get that blood out.

PAULA. Are you kidding? When I tape those promos, I'm gonna look like Jackie at Johnson's swearing in. Move your tail. We've got work to do.

(They exit. SHIFT FOCUS TO –)

Scene Four

(CHEERLEADER PRACTICE. CARMELLE, PEPPER, and ANGELATINA enter carrying gym bags. They all have big bees on their jerseys. They've been practicing, are sweaty and out of breath, but chat excitedly. SINDEE strolls in after them, obviously not having worked out at all. She has a big "A" for "alternate" on her jersey.)

ANGELATINA. Oh, my goodness! I have to tinky winky! I'll be right back.

SINDEE. I'm going to kill myself.

CARMELLE. Don't worry, Sindee. We'll make sure you get a real bee.

SINDEE. You fucking better. You got the stuff?

CARMELLE. Right here. *(Pulls Gatorade bottles and another small bottle out of her bag.)* "Syrup of Ipecac." What's this do?

PEPPER. It makes you puke.

CARMELLE. What are you gonna do with it?

SINDEE. You are gonna put it in that uptight bitch's Gatorade. After she tinky winks, she'll be thirsty and drink it down and then I'll get to be on the squad for tonight's game.

CARMELLE. I'm not sure -

PEPPER. C'mon, Car. Do it for Sindee. She can't because she's the most likely suspect. She can't be anywhere near that bottle just in case.

CARMELLE. What if I get caught?

PEPPER. You just say it was a mistake, you thought it was... I don't know, vanilla or something.

SINDEE. C'mon! She'll be back soon.

(CARMELLE hesitates, then pours Ipecac into one of the bottles of Gatorade. ANGELATINA enters.)

ANGELATINA. Whew! I really had to go! Hey, girls! Mom said I could have a slumber party Friday night. Won't you come?

CARMELLE. Um, no.

PEPPER. I've gotta perm my hair…

SINDEE. We'd love to come (*winks at girls*), wouldn't we, girls?

(*DENCH enters.*)

ANGELATINA. You would?! Hooray!

DENCH. Alright, girls, that was a great workout. Time to hit the showers.

SINDEE. Will you be showering with us today, Ms. Dench?

DENCH. Watch your mouth… alternate. (*Stares SINDEE down.*)

SINDEE. It's like she's licking my pussy with her eyes…

DENCH. (*As she exits:*) And I got twenty-twenty vision, Sandstone…

ANGELATINE. Weird! Wow, I'm parched!

SINDEE. And I'm… have to be somewhere else. I'll be right back. (*Exits.*)

PEPPER. So hey, Carmelle was so nice and brought everyone Gatorade today.

CARMELLE. Oh, yeah, want some?

ANGELATINA. Oh, my gosh that is so generous! Thank you!

(*CARMELLE should be holding two bottles of Gatorade by this point. ANGELATINA grabs what is obviously the wrong BOTTLE— i.e., no Ipecac—and chugs the whole thing. As she drinks, CARMELLE and PEPPER realize she's drinking the wrong bottle. SINDEE enters.*)

PEPPER. (*To ANGELATINA.*) Uh, wait! Don't you want some more?

SINDEE. How's that juice? Stupid…Gimme that. (*Grabs the other Gatorade bottle [with Ipecac] and immediately starts chugging it.*)

CARMELLE. Wait -

(*PEPPER elbows her, SINDEE drinks the juice. Her eyes bulge. She gags.*)

SINDEE. You are dead. (*She runs off. We hear vomiting.*)

ANGELATINA. What was that all about?

(*The other two giggle despite themselves.*)

PEPPER. Nothing. Let's hit the showers.

(*The three exit. SHIFT FOCUS TO –*)

Scene Five

(*OUTSIDE THE DINER. VERA walking her dog. CHARLENE approaches.*)

VERA. Hello, Charlene!

CHARLENE. What's that?

VERA. This? It's Poopsie!

CHARLENE. What?

VERA. A dog, you silly noodle. His name is Poopsie.

CHARLENE. Poopsie?

VERA. Yeah. We named him that because he, you know, a lot. I have to take him out three times a day.

CHARLENE. I certainly hope he never gets off his leash.

VERA. Oh, certainly not. We had a bad experience with one of our little boys who got off his leash.

CHARLENE. (*Hopefully:*) Oh? (*Realization:*) Oh. You mean a dog.

VERA. Yes. You see, we got Angelatina a puppy for her tenth birthday. It was a cocker spaniel. Not too big, not too small. Beautiful golden color. It was the runt of the litter, and the breeder said he would need lots of love to get over being taken from its mother. And if there's one thing Angelatina is full of, it's love. So we went to the breeder on the morning before her b-day party, picked up Scooter — that was his name, Scooter — and put him in a big box with lots of holes in it and a big pink bow and drove right home for the party. All of Angelatina's friends were there, streamers everywhere, cake, the whole number. We set the box down in front of "A" — sometimes we call her "A" for short — and she had this look in her eyes, like "Could it be?" Like she had some sixth sense, as if she were psychically connected somehow to Scooter. Oh, it was magical. And she opened the box, and out jumped Scooter and he ran across the yard and into the street and got hit by a car and died. Angelatina's father was so panicked he ran out into the street and slipped in the blood and fell and hit his head on the pavement, and then, all woozy, staggered back into this screaming group of children covered in dog intestines. Well, I won't go into the whole mess except to say that the cake was ruined and very soon after, Mr. Vindechi left us. So no, he never ever gets off his leash.

CHARLENE. What? Sorry. I've got this song in my head and I just can't concentrate. Gotta go. Picking up lunch.

VERA. Oh, bye.

(*VERA exits with dog. CHARLENE crosses as we SHIFT FOCUS TO –*)

Scene Six

(*DINER. RUBY is working.*)

RUBY. Hey there, honey! The usual?

CHARLENE. Yeah, and pack it to go. I gotta get back and water the garden before "Pontificate With Paula."

RUBY. Water? Don't tell me you're takin' this "How Green" contest seriously?

CHARLENE. Of course I am!

RUBY. But you know you'll win. Nobody else gives half a crap about this thing but you. They'll all pay the entrance fee just 'cause it's a good cause.

CHARLENE. News flash, Ruby. That Vindechi woman will take this seriously. You know how much she wants to fit in. She'll be out there at midnight trimmin' her bush with a tweezers if she thinks it'll help her win.

RUBY. (*Snickers.*) Which bush? (*Cracks herself up.*) Ah ha ha ha! Double entender!

CHARLENE. What? Oh, Ruby. That mouth.

RUBY. Well, it might be nice for her to win. Maybe it would give the Auxiliary a kick in the underpants.

CHARLENE. And what do you mean by that?

RUBY. I mean that it might be nice to have some new blood in the governing body of the Auxiliary. Look, Char, we're friends and all, but I gotta tell ya — sangria and the stories every Tuesday is fine for a while, but we need something new. Some sorta challenge or something. Kathy and I talked about it last night —

CHARLENE. Oh, so you and Kathy talked.

RUBY. Well, yeah. We do have conversations without you in the room every once in a while. And we decided there might be a need for a change.

CHARLENE. Uh huh.

RUBY. And, well, that's about it.

CHARLENE. Oh, it is, is it? Well, I have a little "it" to add. How about we up the stakes on this little contest that nobody seems to be taking seriously.

RUBY. What do you mean?

CHARLENE. I mean, how about whoever wins this little botanical competition becomes the new president and chair of the Tubbville Ladies Auxiliary?

RUBY. Oh, well —

CHARLENE. Oh, well what?

RUBY. Well, I mean it doesn't have to –

CHARLENE. Put your garden where your mouth is, honey. Because as social chair for the Tubbville Ladies Auxiliary I hereby declare that the winner of the "How Green Was My Valley" contest will take over as president and acting chair, effective immediately after the contest concludes. So if you want a change, you can make it happen. Capiche?

RUBY. Cap — ... Yes.

CHARLENE. Good. Now hand over my lunch.

(*RUBY hands over an impossibly small [or huge] package. KATHY enters.*)

CHARLENE. Adios. (*She passes KATHY as she exits.*) How's that garden comin' along, darling?
KATHY. Garden? Oh, that. Okay, I guess.
CHARLENE. Glad to hear it. (*Exits.*)
KATHY. What's up her rumpus? Besides the usual?
RUBY. Come on in the back. I'll tell you over lunch.

(*They exit. SHIFT FOCUS TO –*)

Scene Seven

(*ANGELATINA'S BEDROOM. Slumber party. ANGELATINA, SINDEE, CARMELLE, PEPPER and VERA enter excitedly chatting and laughing. The girls should have pillows, stuffed animals and their diaries.*)

VERA. This is so exciting! A slumber party! A rite of passage for every young American girl.
ANGELATINA. American? Don't you suppose they have sleepovers in the Soviet Union?
VERA. With the recent fall of communism I would suppose yes, the former Union of Soviet Socialist Republics would be very receptive to the idea of a pajama party.
ANGELATINA. Thank goodness! No girl, no matter what her social or political background, should be denied the excitement of staying up all night with some of her closest friends.
PEPPER. You have a wicked nice house, Mrs. Vindechi.
VERA. Well, thank you.
CARMELLE. Did you really sew all of the comforters and pillowcases for all of the bedroom sets?
VERA. That I did.
SINDEE. Well, they're just beautiful!
VERA. Thank you, Sindee. That was very nice of you to say.
SINDEE. Yes, it was, wasn't it?
VERA. So, what do you girls have planned for this evening?
ANGELATINA. Well, we're going to have some snacks, and then play some records and dance, and then have a séance —
VERA. Ooooh…
ANGELATINA. — and then we're going to share some of our most private secrets from our diaries.
VERA. Sounds like you girls have everything all planned out.
SINDEE. That we do.

VERA. You know, we used to do some pretty crazy stuff when we were kids.

SINDEE. (*Under her breath:*) Like inventing the wheel...

VERA. Excuse me?

SINDEE. Like what?

VERA. Well, the far out thing we used to do — do kids still say that? "Far out"? — was, well, freeze each other's brassieres.

ANGELATINA. (*Giggling:*) Mother, stop it!

VERA. I won't! That's exactly what we did. Take the bra, dip it in water, and put it in the freezer overnight!

ANGELATINA. Oh, mother! You never told me that!

VERA. And I'm sure you can imagine my mother trying to control a group of frozen bra-ed teenagers at seven a.m. Saturday morning.

ANGELATINA. Grandma! Oh, my goodness! Girls, isn't that crazy?

SINDEE / PEPPER / CARMELLE. (*Too enthusiastically:*) Hee hee hee, crazy... etc.

SINDEE. Insane, actually.

VERA. Time for bed. Well, for me anyway. I'll see you girls in the morning. 'Night.

ALL GIRLS. 'Night.

ANGELATINA. (*With a wink*) Mother, could you clear out the freezer?

VERA. What...? Oh, of course... (*Wink.*)

(*They start a laugh. VERA claps twice, the lights dim, and she exits.*)

ANGELATINA. What shall we do first? The séance? Now that my mother mentioned her, I would like to contact my grandmother. I've missed her so much since she passed away. She was my favorite. She was fat, just like grandmas are supposed to be. She used to bake every Wednesday, and every week we would have special time when she would braid my hair and tell me stories about the Depression. You know, they didn't have much money then. That's why they called it a depression.

SINDEE. (*A beat.*) Where the hell are the snacks?

ANGELATINA. Oh! Where's my head? I'll go get the snacks, and you stay right here.

SINDEE / PEPPER / CARMELLE. Okay, just go! Etc.

ANGELATINA. You stay right here, and I'll be in there.

SINDEE / PEPPER / CARMELLE. Okay, yes, go! Just go. We'll be here! Etc.

ANGELATINA. But I'll be right back. (*She exits.*)

SINDEE. Oh, my God for fuck's sake just go!

CARMELLE. Now what?

SINDEE. We get this diary thing going. Then later, while dumbass is freezing our bras, we swipe her diary. I paid one of the forensics geeks to read select passages Monday morning during the school announcements.

PEPPER. That's awful. (*They laugh.*) Here she comes.

(*ANGELATINA enters.*)

ANGELATINA. Okay, Diet Coke and Snackwells!

PEPPER. Great. Hey, let's get right to the diaries!

SINDEE. Subtle.

CARMELLE. Yeah, let's. Who wants to go first?

ANGELATINA. How about Pepper since she suggested it?

PEPPER. Oh, okay. Let's see... I know. You give me a page number and I'll read it. Between one and one hundred seventy-three.

ANGELATINA. One hundred and two.

PEPPER. Okay... (*Reads:*) "...and the store security must have seen me, Dear Diary, because before I knew it, I was hauled into the back of the store and asked to empty my bag. I was so embarrassed. When I pulled out the lipsticks, the store security called the police. I knew I had to act fast, so I pretended to start crying. By the time the cops got there I was in 'hysterics,' so they just gave me a lecture and let me go. I went straight over to —"

CARMELLE / SINDEE. Keep going!

PEPPER. Uh, uh. She said page one hundred and two, and that's all that's on that page. You'll have to wait for next turn.

ANGELATINA. You got caught shoplifting?

PEPPER. Yeah.

ANGELATINA. You shoplifted?

CARMELLE. It's no big whoop. Everybody does it.

SINDEE. Don't you shoplift, Angelatina?

ANGELATINA. Uh...sure...sometimes.

PEPPER. Okay, Carmelle. You're next.

CARMELLE. Okay, between one and seven hundred twenty-six. (*She pulls out a huge diary.*)

PEPPER. Three hundred and six.

CARMELLE. Okay. This is from Tuesday. (*Reads:*) "Today's affirmation - Not everyone is looking at your thighs. They are looking at your brain by way of your knees. Now on to the good stuff, Diary. I am in love. L-U-V, love. With Zach.

SINDEE / PEPPER / ANGELATINA. (*Shocked or enthusiastic reactions.*)

CARMELLE. 'Z' is for the zero times he is mean to me. 'A' is for the A+ he gets on a date with me. 'C' is for 'completely.' Used in a sentence — 'I am completely in love with Zach.' 'H' is for Heath Bar Crunch, the kind of ice cream we had on our first date. I could write his name a million times. Zach, Zach, Zach, Zach, Zach, Zach, Zach, Zach, Zach, Zach, Zach, Zach, Zach, Zach, Zach, Zach..."

SINDEE. Okay, okay! Jeez!

ANGELATINA. I thought it was romantic, Carmelle.

CARMELLE. Oh, thanks.

SINDEE. My turn. Between one and... twelve.

PEPPER. Hey!

SINDEE. I just started this volume.

PEPPER. Fine. Eight.

SINDEE. Alright. (*Reads:*) "Hurt my ankle in aerobics today, so I won't be able to go on that date with — " (*Pause*) "Eddie Bryan —"

(*The girls all laugh.*)

CARMELLE. Oh my God! You were going to go out with Ed Bryant? He is the hugest geek mus grande at Susan B. Anthony High!

SINDEE. (*Continuing, sulkily:*) "He said he'd pay, so I figured why not."

PEPPER. That's it?

SINDEE. It's a short page.

CARMELLE. Okay, Angelatina. You're next. (*CARMELLE laughs. The other two shush her.*)

ANGELATINA. Okay. Pick between one and two hundred forty-seven.

CARMELLE. Fifty-eight. (*She laughs again. They shush her.*)

ANGELATINA. (*Reads:*) "We haven't seen him for months, and I have to draw the conclusion that he is not coming back. Mother cries almost every night, and I try to comfort her, but inside I'm crying, too. Can anyone see this sunny façade for what it is? A mask? Inside I'm dying, but on the outside I must keep a smiling persona because that's what the world wants. No one wants to be confronted with the reality of emotions, at least the bad ones, like anger, or sorrow, or pity, or jealousy, or grumpy, or persnickety or anything like that. I'm sorry, Elizabeth — " That's what I call my diary, it makes it more personal that way. (*Reads:*) "I'm sorry, Elizabeth. I've gotten off the track. I just know that if I keep a happy face that soon mother will be all better, and then I can cry alone and come back to the world a better person for it."

SINDEE. (*A beat:*) Okay, time for that séance!

ANGELATINA. Let's do it in the rec room. I feel more psychic energy there.

PEPPER. Okay. Why don't you bring the snacks and we'll get the rest of the stuff.

ANGELATINA. Okay. Meet you there. (*She exits.*)

SINDEE. Okay, you grab her diary. I've already paid Betty, so just drop it off Monday morning and split.

PEPPER. Okay.

CARMELLE / SINDEE. Here we come, Angelatina!

(*SINDEE and CARMELLE pick up some stuff and exit. PEPPER picks up ANGELATINA's diary, and then spies SINDEE's. She holds both of them up—they are exactly the same. She shrugs, and exits. SHIFT FOCUS TO –*)

Scene Eight

(*VINDECHI HOME / GARDEN AREA. VERA is tending her garden and singing something to herself. ANGELATINA enters and does a little cheer.*)

ANGELATINA. Hooray, they like me!

VERA. Well, what's that all about?

ANGELATINA. The slumber party was a success! They like me! They really like me!

VERA. Yay team!

ANGELATINA. I've finally been accepted by my peers!

VERA. You see? What goes around comes around. You know that.

ANGELATINA. Like a Ferris wheel?

VERA. Or a merry-go-round?

ANGELATINA. Or a blender?

VERA. Or a rotisserie microwave. (*They both laugh.*) That's fun! Now see? It's not that bad.

ANGELATINA. I guess not.

VERA. Why don't you go in and make us some raspberry iced tea, and then come out and help me with the garden. I think we got a winner here.

ANGELATINA. Okay. Thanks, Mom.

(*She exits. VERA tends her garden. KATHY enters and begins tending her garden.*)

VERA. Howdy-do! Kathy!

KATHY. Vera!

VERA. How's the green valley coming?

KATHY. Oh… fine. Did you hear about the new rules?

VERA. That I did. And I'm gonna give you gals a run for your money.

(*RUBY enters in her garden.*)

VERA. Hidey-ho! Ruby!

RUBY. Hey, Vera. How's it hangin'?

VERA. How's…? Oh, you!

KATHY. It feels like these row houses get closer together every year.

(*CHARLENE enters and tends her garden.*)

VERA. Ello-hay, Arlene-shay!

CHARLENE. What?

VERA. Ig-pay Atin-lay. Pig Latin, silly! It's fun! You just take the first consonant from each word and put it at the end followed by the sound "ay."

(*SINDEE and ANGELATINA have both entered from different parts of the stage.*)

ANGELATINA. Mom loves cunning linguistics, like Pig Latin, oooh, and the Name Game!

VERA. The Name Game! Hey! Let's do "Vera"!

VERA / ANGELATINA. "Vera, Vera, bo bera! Banana fana fo fera! Mi my mo mera! Vera!"

SINDEE. Mother, make them stop! They're scaring me!

ANGELATINA. Let's do "Chuck!"

VERA / ANGELATINA. "Chuck, Chuck, bo buck! Banana fana fo -"

VERA. Whoops! That's enough of that!

CHARLENE. I'll say.

ANGELATINA Would anyone like some iced tea? It's raspberry.

KATHY. Sure.

RUBY. I'll take some.

ANGELATINA. Hello, Sindee, Mrs. Sandstone. Tea?

(*VERA's dog comes out barking.*)

CHARLENE. Holy shit! It's attacking! (*She shoves SINDEE in front of the dog.*)

VERA. No, no! He's not attacking! He's just frisky! Poopsie, now stop barking!

KATHY. Puppy!

RUBY. Hey, ya mangy little mutt!

KATHY. Come over here, you two. Pet the dog.

SINDEE. I hate dogs.

CHARLENE. (*Petting SINDEE.*) Good girl.

ANGELATINA. Mother, let's invite everyone in for coffee and snacks.

VERA. My little banana bread! A hostess in the making! Would anyone like to come in for coffee and cake? (*Dead silence as RUBY and KATHY look uneasily at CHARLENE.*) I have chocolate swirl bundt.

RUBY. (*Struggles, as CHARLENE has found her weakness. Finally:*) Well, why not.

KATHY. Oh, okay. Yes!

VERA. You will? Oh, my goodness, we're havin' a little hen party!

CHARLENE. Cluck, cluck.

VERA. Charlene? Sindee?

CHARLENE. Humph. No. We have a garden to attend to.
VERA. Oh. Well. Maybe next time, then.
CHARLENE. Maybe.
VERA. Come on, girls! Hup, two, three, four!

(*VERA, RUBY and KATHY exit.*)

ANGELATINA. Bye Sindee!
SINDEE. (*Mocking:*) Bye!
ANGELATINA. Thanks for the slumber party.
SINDEE. (*Mocking:*) My pleasure!
ANGELATINA. See you at school! (*She exits.*)
SINDEE. (*Mocking:*) Monday morning, bright and early! Ooh! I'd like to kick her where it counts!
CHARLENE. You should have thought of that before that little snip took your place on the cheerleading squad. Kick her where it counts. I'll show you "kick her where it counts." Pay close attention, young lady. (*She goes over to the dog, which growls at her.*) Shut up, you little toilet seat cover in the making. (*She unties his leash. The dog just stands there, barking.*) Move it, fleabag!

(*She kicks or throws the dog into the street. We hear the sound of a car hitting the dog.*)

KATHY. (*Off*) What was that?
RUBY. (*Off*) Sounded like a car crash...
VERA. (*Off*) Oh, my goodness! POOPSIE!
CHARLENE. Kick them where it counts.

(*CHARLENE exits followed by a horrified SINDEE. SHIFT FOCUS TO –*)

Scene Nine

(*"PONTIFICATE WITH PAULA." TERRI enters and, using the theater audience as the studio audience, explains the format of the show. This should be very loose and partially improvised if appropriate.*)

TERRI. Hello, everyone. Welcome to "Pontificate With Paula." I'm Terri, the floor manager. How is everyone today? (*If no answer, she should work them until they do.*) Now, your host, Paulo DeMarcato, hates spontaneous outbursts or questions, so we've devised a little system of call and response. First off, we have the "Applause" sign. When I hold it up, you applaud. Very simple. Let's try it, shall we? (*She holds up the "Applause" card for a microsecond.*) Good, good. Second, we have some very simple response cards. All you have to do is, when I hold up the card, you read what it says. Okay? (*Holds up a card that says "Okay." The audience responds.*) Great! Oh, looks like it's time to go. Ladies, can I get you in please? Can we get the guests in their seats?

(*TERRI improvises guiding VERA, JANET, and GRETCHEN in to their seats. PAULA enters and positions herself for the beginning of the show.*)

TERRI. Cue the music. We'll go in 5, 4, 3, …

(*Theme music plays. Two, one, and on the air.*)

PAULA. Welcome. Welcome in from the storm outside. I'm Paula, and this is our time. Today we have some guests. Friends, really. All of whom…who? Whom?

TERRI. Whom.

PAULA. Who. All of who have suffered a loss. An irreplaceable loss. The loss…(*Reading the prompter:*) of a pet. (*To Terri:*) Are you fucking kidding me? (*Recovers.*) The loss of a pet. Let's meet them, shall we?

(*All CROWD responses are written on cards held by TERRI.*)

CROWD. Yes.

PAULA. Everyone, meet Janet.

CROWD. Hello, Janet.

PAULA. Janet Michaels, you're from —

JANET. But… but… wait… You said you weren't going to use my last name!

PAULA. Well, what the fuck! Come on! You're holding up my show!

JANET. But you said —

PAULA. Alright, alright, alright, alright, ALRIGHT! Fucking A! It was only a cat, for shit's sake!

JANET. But she was all I had —

PAULA. Terri! I need a name!

TERRI. (*Rushes on.*) Jane. (*Rushes off.*)

PAULA. Alright, Jane…et, why don't you tell us your story?

JANET. Well — (*she breaks down*)

PAULA. Here. (*Throws a box of tissues roughly at JANET.*) Moving on. Gretchen. I assume you have no problem with your real name?

GRETCHEN. No, ma'am.

PAULA. Uh huh. So. Gretchen. Tell us.

GRETCHEN. Well, actually, there's been a wee mistake.

PAULA. A what?

GRETCHEN. A mistake. You see, I just thought Chuckie was dead.

PAULA. What?

GRETCHEN. Yes, see, he just woke up and he was fine. See? (*GRETCHEN pulls out a bloody dog carcass she uses as a puppet.*) Woof! Bow-wow! Ruff ruff! Grrr! Woof Woof! Aoooh!

PAULA. Gretchen, you have your hand up that dog's ass.
GRETCHEN. No, I don't.
PAULA. Yes. You. Do.
GRETCHEN. No, I don't.
PAULA. Gretchen —
GRETCHEN. Careful. He bites. Grrr —

(*PAULA snatches the dog off GRETCHEN's hand, throws it on the ground and grinds her heel into it. GRETCHEN makes dog-getting-hurt noises.*)

PAULA. Terri! Get out here and get rid of this thing!

(*TERRI rushes out and takes the dog off. GRETCHEN makes dog noises that seem to fade as the dog goes further away.*)

PAULA. (*Seething:*) Vera.
VERA. Paula.
PAULA. Have you something to share with us?

VERA. My dog was killed.
PAULA. And?
VERA. It was very sad.
PAULA. I'm thinking we can do better than that, Vera.
VERA. (*Sighs*) This is my second little boy who has met his death prematurely under the wheels of a car. The first time it happened I thought I'd never get over it. You see, it wasn't just losing a pet; it was losing a member of the family. I know that sounds ludicrous. It did to me before I had my first. But they are family. They have personalities, and you get used to them being there for you. You get used to them listening when no one else will, or you don't want anyone else to. They know when you're happy… or sad. (*Begins to cry.*) And they can hold a family together with their little wagging tail. I found that out the hard way. After a horrible incident where we lost our first, Mr. Vindechi left the family. He just stopped loving me or something. I'll never know, because he just disappeared leaving me to raise our daughter alone. And now… now I'm afraid it will happen again. I've lost my little one, and now I'm afraid I'll lose my daughter… and I couldn't live through that again. I'm sorry… (*Breaks down sobbing.*)
PAULA. (*A beat.*) YES! THAT'S what I meant when I asked you if you had something to share, you pathetic nimrods! That's a story! Not that Muppet freak show! (*Mocking:*) "Please don't use my name or I'll have to kill myself over my fucking cat!!" Get some guts and do it, baby! Do us all a favor!

(*JANET rushes off.*)

PAULA. What are you looking at?
GRETCHEN. Woof! Grrr —
PAULA. Get her out of here!

(*TERRI drags GRETCHEN off, growling all the way.*)

PAULA. (*Off-handed:*) That's the end of the program goodbye.

(*Theme music. Off the air.*)
PAULA. That was great! Who wrote that?
VERA. What?
PAULA. You really pulled this show out of the crapper today.
VERA. Thank you... I think.
PAULA. I... whoa, this is strange.
VERA. What?
PAULA. For some reason, I'm feeling like I should do something nice for you now. Wow. That's weird.
VERA. Nice? Like what?
PAULA. I don't know. You tell me.
VERA. Well, I... wait a minute. I do have an idea.

(*They exit. SHIFT FOCUS TO –*)

Scene Ten

(*CLASSROOM / SCHOOL OFFICE. SINDEE, PEPPER, and CARMELLE enter and take their seats.*)

PEPPER. That was fab how your Mom killed that hosebag's dog and everything.
CARMELLE. I don't know. I feel kinda sorry for the dog.
SINDEE. Shut up, you idiots! You wanna get my Mom thrown in jail? That stupid mutt ran out into the street and that's it.
PEPPER. Sorry.
SINDEE. Gimme a smoke.
PEPPER. I don't have any.
SINDEE. What?
PEPPER. Well, I quit.
SINDEE. What? What the fuck is wrong with you two?
PEPPER. I was having shortness of breath —
SINDEE. Carmelle, fork over! (*She snatches a smoke from CARMELLE.*) "I feel sorry for the dog. I quit smoking." You two better get your fucking act together, or it's over.
CARMELLE. What do you mean?
SINDEE. I mean you two stupid skanks will be out of the most popular clique in the school.

CARMELLE. You wouldn't!

SINDEE. Try me.

PEPPER. Carmelle, gimme a smoke.

SINDEE. That's better. Carmelle?

CARMELLE. I... um... hate that dog...

SINDEE. I'm not sure I believe you, Carmelle. I think you're faking it.

CARMELLE. I'm not! Serious! Really, I hate that cute little dog!

SINDEE. Uh, huh...

PEPPER. I think she's lying.

CARMELLE. Pepper!

SINDEE. You know, I heard Carmelle was secretly going out with Brett Cooper.

CARMELLE. Sindee, stop it!

PEPPER. Yeah, I heard she let him feel her up.

CARMELLE. Stop it! Somebody will hear!

SINDEE. I heard it was Brett Cooper and Jack.

CARMELLE. Jack who?

SINDEE / PEPPER. The custodian!

CARMELLE. STOP IT! I do hate her! I'll prove it!

(*BETTY enters the school office area and switches on the intercom.*)

BETTY. (*Via intercom:*) May I have your attention please for the morning announcements?

PEPPER. Where's Angelatina?

SINDEE. It doesn't matter. She'll find out about it.

BETTY. (*Via intercom:*) There will be a Science Club meeting after school today in Room 219. Will both members of the club please be prompt as you have a lot of material to cover. All students who have not received their student activities cards must report to the office sometime today. The pep band will be playing pop standards for your enjoyment during pre-game ceremonies at tonight's game, so please come early. Mr. Berg says an empty gym causes an echo effect that throws off the band's timing, as evidenced by their pre-match show at the girls' volleyball game last week. And now for something special. (*Reads from SINDEE's diary:*) "Hurt my ankle in aerobics today, so I won't be able to go on that date with Eddie Bryant. He said he'd pay, so why not?"

PEPPER. Oops.

BETTY. (*Via intercom, reads:*) "It's too bad, too, because the last date we went on ended up in his garage. I've done it in the back seat of a car, but not on the hood. Eddie may be a geek on the outside, but on the inside, he's all man, if you know what I'm saying. One of my knees actually hit my face and gave me a black eye. After an experience like that I can truly say I am a woman. I am a slave to his manhood. A willing slave. Pull me by my hair, caveman, and treat me like the loathsome animal I was meant to be. Knock me over the head and then rock my world. And with that I leave you, Diary, to ice my wounded ankle." That was a passage from the diary of (*Flips to first page.*) Sindee Sandstone. (*Realizing what she has done:*) Uh… this will be the last time you hear my voice, as I expect to be murdered within twenty-four hours. Goodbye! (*Exits.*)

SINDEE. You are fucking dead —

(*DENCH enters.*)

DENCH. Alright! Quiet down and take your seats.

SINDEE. What are you doing here? This is Our Ever-Changing Bodies, not gym.

DENCH. I'm subbing. Ms. Julian is out with her lady friend who makes a visit once a month to her basement apartment to replenish her secret garden.

SINDEE. What?

DENCH. She's having her period. No lip, Sandstone. Plant it. We've got special visitors today. Angelatina, would you like to come in and introduce your guest?

(*ANGELATINA enters.*)

ANGELATINA. Hi everybody! I'm so nervous! Today, I have a special treat I'd like to share with you and the whole school. It's a woman whom I have admired for a long time now. I… well, I don't know what else to say. I'm sure you'll all know her. Ms. Paula DeMarcato!

(*PAULA enters. The girls go nuts.*)

SINDEE. Holy shit!

PAULA. Hello, ladies!

ANGELATINA. Ms. DeMarcato —

PAULA. Paula, please.

ANGELATINA. I mean Paula Please… oops! (*Giggles*) Paula agreed to come to school and take questions during lunch period.

PAULA. This is quite a lovely school you have here. Anything fun planned for the students coming up?

DENCH. Yes, actually. The Spring Formal is next month. We'll be electing a court in the next week or so.

PAULA. Really?

DENCH. Yes. We usually have some sort of local celeb pick the queen and the court, then crown them at the dance.

ANGELATINA. Couldn't you do it, Ms. De — I mean, Paula?

PAULA. Well, I don't know —

DENCH. Angelatina, Rachel Winters from that cooking show, "A Wok On The Wild Side," will be disappointed —

PAULA. I'll do it!

ANGELATINA. Hooray!

DENCH. Well, I'm the head of the committee, so I guess I have the authority to appoint you to the position. It's all yours, Paula.

ANGELATINA. I'm so excited!

PAULA. Me too, honey. Me, too. Now, as my first official act as the selection committee, I'm going to select the Queen of the court.

DENCH. Now?!

ANGELATINA. Oh, my goodness!

PAULA. That's part of the deal, right?

DENCH. Well, I guess so...

PAULA. So as the selector for the Spring Formal, I choose Angelatina Vindechi as the Queen of the court!

SINDEE. WHAT!!?

ANGELATINA. (*Stunned:*) Oh, my goodness...

PAULA. I need to run. (*Exits.*)

ANGELATINA. (*Weak:*) Ms. Dench, I've got to lie down.

DENCH. Come on, dear. We'll take you to the sick room.

(*DENCH helps ANGELATINA out. SINDEE just stands there, ominously quiet.*)

PEPPER. Sindee? Sindee, listen to me. Before you do something rash...

CARMELLE. I'm sure there's something in the rules against this —

SINDEE. That slutbitchslitcumguzzlingfuckbagWHORE!!

PEPPER. Sindee —

SINDEE. Who does that bitch think she is?!

CARMELLE. She's lost it! Run!

SINDEE. Don't move. That bitch can't be Queen! She's a sophomore. I'm a senior!

CARMELLE. What do we do?

SINDEE. Do you hate her? Do you hate her? ANSWER ME!!

PEPPER / CARMELLE. Yes, I hate her! etc.

SINDEE. And you said you wanted to prove it to me, right?

CARMELLE. Um, right.

SINDEE. Well, now is your chance. Come on!

PEPPER. Sindee, wait!

CARMELLE. You look really pretty!

(*SINDEE storms out with PEPPER and CARMELLE following and trying to calm her down. SHIFT FOCUS TO –*)

Scene Eleven

(*ON THE STREET. PAULA with TERRI.*)

PAULA. I must admit, that was one of my more brilliant moves.
TERRI. What now?
PAULA. I just named a girl despised by her classmates the Queen of the Spring Formal.
TERRI. Why is that brilliant?
PAULA. Because, stupid, now there will be a lot of in-fighting among the students, it's likely to get violent, and I'll be there to expose the whole rotten, delicious scandal.
TERRI. Wow. Neat.
PAULA. Come on, Terri. I'm feeling charitable. Let's go get a pedicure. I'm sure those hooves could use a little filing down. My treat.
TERRI. Your treat? You must be happy.

(*They exit. SHIFT FOCUS TO –*)

Scene Twelve

(*SICK ROOM. DENCH escorts ANGELATINA in to see the NURSE who enters from another door.*)

ANGELATINA. I'm so embarrassed. (*She passes out onto the floor.*)
DENCH. I think she just needs to walk it off.
NURSE. (*Excited:*) No, I think she's really sick! Let's get her on the bed.
DENCH. I got the top.

(*DENCH's hands find their way to ANGELATINA'S breasts as they heft her onto the bed. DENCH starts unbuttoning ANGELATINA's shirt.*)

NURSE. I'm afraid I'm going to have to ask you to leave.
DENCH. What? Don't you need me to help her get undressed?
NURSE. No, thank you. (*Pushes DENCH out.*)
DENCH. (*Off.*) I hate you!
NURSE. This definitely calls for a speculum!

(*NURSE exits. SINDEE, PEPPER, and CARMELLE enter the sick room.*)

CARMELLE. Sindee, what's going on?
SINDEE. Shut up!
PEPPER. Yeah, shut up.
SINDEE. You shut up, too.
PEPPER. Shut up!

SINDEE. Everybody shut up! Are you ready, Carmelle?

CARMELLE. For what?

SINDEE. Is she still out?

PEPPER. Cold.

SINDEE. Good. Here. (*She pulls out a gun and holds it out to CARMELLE.*)

PEPPER. Sindee!

SINDEE. Take it, Carmelle.

PEPPER. Sindee, what are you doing?!

SINDEE. Take it.

CARMELLE. I can't!

SINDEE. That's not what I heard from Brett Cooper.

PEPPER. Sindee, stop it!

SINDEE. And Jack. Did you blow him in the broom closet?

PEPPER. Sindee, this is too far!

SINDEE. Did you let him feel you up?

CARMELLE. No —

SINDEE. Did you let him finger you?

PEPPER. Stop it!

SINDEE. Take the gun, Carmelle. (*She forces the gun into CARMELLE's hands.*) Now get over there and finish that bitch off.

PEPPER. Carmelle —

SINDEE. Come on, Carmelle. Get in there. I've got fifty friends outside that door who will swear they saw you suck Jack's dick. Every fucking person in this school will swear that you're pregnant by that freak —

CARMELLE. STOP IT!!

SINDEE. — and you can kiss all your friends goodbye when I tell them he bent you over —

CARMELLE. STOP IT!!

SINDEE. — and fucked you up the ass!!

(*CARMELLE shoots ANGELATINA, emptying the gun.*)

SINDEE / CARMELLE / PEPPER. (*Screaming:*) AAAIIIEEE!!!

SINDEE. Run!

(*They run out. NURSE enters.*)

NURSE. Darling? Angie? (*Shakes her.*) Oh no...

(*ANGELATINA's body falls to the floor in a bloody heap. The NURSE screams. BLACKOUT.*)

END OF ACT ONE

ACT TWO

Scene Thirteen

(*VINDECHI HOME. Gathering after the funeral. VERA, KATHY, RUBY, CHARLENE, MS. DENCH, SINDEE, CARMELLE, PEPPER, PAULA, and TERRI all sit with empty plates, silently grieving in their own way, while CHARLENE eats an entire piece of cake, first bite to last. Finally —*)

CHARLENE. Ya got any more cake?
VERA. (*Dully:*) In the kitchen.
KATHY. (*A beat, then:*) The service was beautiful.
ALL. Yes, lovely, etc.
SINDEE. I loved it.
VERA. Yes…
RUBY. That Father Hoolihan certainly is a hunk of granite.
KATHY. And how.
RUBY. I wonder how he looks without that collar— (*Notices VERA isn't responding.*) Beautiful service.
VERA. Yes…

(*CHARLENE enters from kitchen with an empty pitcher.*)

CHARLENE. I'm going to mix up some more Crystal Light, okay? Vera?
VERA. Huh?
CHARLENE. Okay? The Crystal Light?
VERA. Sure…
CHARLENE. Honestly. (*Exits.*)
DENCH. Vera, I just want to say — and this isn't just because she's dead and all — your Angelatina was a very special girl. She was a wonderful addition to the cheerleading squad.
SINDEE. Yes, she was. Wasn't she, girls?
PEPPER. Yes.
CARMELLE. Uh… yeah…
VERA. That's very nice. You know, she never felt like she fit in, so it's so nice to spend this sad, sad day with some of her true friends. (*Cries.*)
KATHY. Come on, Ruby; let's pick up some of these dishes.

(*RUBY and KATHY pick up stuff and exit.*)

PAULA. (*To Terry:*) This will make a great fucking show.
TERRI. What?!
PAULA. Think we can pump up the relationship between the gym teacher and the girl?
TERRI. The gym teacher? You mean…?

PAULA. Keep your ear to the ground. What time is it?

TERRI. Four thirty.

PAULA. Shit. We've got a taping in two hours. Let's see if we can stir something up.

SINDEE. (*To Carmelle:*) What the hell is wrong with you?

PEPPER. Come on, Sindee. Lay off.

SINDEE. Don't you tell me what to do.

PEPPER. Why not?

SINDEE. Shut up and watch. It should happen any minute.

(*POLICEWOMAN bursts in.*)

POLICEWOMAN. Hello, ladies.

DENCH. Holy shit! A lady police officer!

POLICEWOMAN. Anybody else here?

DENCH. Yes. Ladies! Come in here!

(*Everyone enters.*)

POLICEWOMAN. Is there a Carmelle Constantine present?

CARMELLE. (*Scared:*) Yes. Here.

POLICEWOMAN. You are under arrest for the murder of Angelatina Vindechi!

ALL. (*Aghast hubbub.*)

(*POLICEWOMAN immediately starts beating CARMELLE with her police baton. After beating her in front of the gathered crowd for a bit [to loud and vocal horrified reactions] the POLICEWOMAN beats CARMELLE out the door as they exit.*)

VERA. Oh, my goodness… (*Faints dead away.*)

PAULA. Hooray! … I mean… How horrible! Gotta go! Terri, come on!

(*PAULA and TERRI exit.*)

RUBY. Let's get her to the bedroom.

(*RUBY, KATHY, and MS. DENCH improvise pulling a woozy VERA to her feet and leading her out.*)

PEPPER. I gotta go. (*Exits.*)

(*SINDEE turns to her mother.*)

SINDEE. Kick 'em where it counts.

(*She saunters out. SHIFT FOCUS TO –*)

Scene Fourteen

(*STREET. CARMELLE being escorted by POLICEWOMAN with PAULA and TERRI hounding her. The POLICEWOMAN switches her police hat with a REPORTER's hat with a "Press" card in the brim.*)

REPORTER. Is it true your parents are divorced?
TERRI. Were you involved with the school janitor?
REPORTER. I have your signature here on a petition to allow shorts in school. Do you consider this subversive?
PAULA. Do you deny the rumor that you have had an intimate relationship with Lila Dench, Susan B. Anthony High School gym teacher and cheerleading coach?
TERRI / REPORTER. Ooooohhh…
CARMELLE. What?! I love Ms. Dench. She's my favorite teacher —
PAULA / TERRI / REPORTER. Aha!
CARMELLE. Wait! Stop twisting my words!

(*PAULA and TERRI exit. REPORTER changes back to the POLICEWOMAN. She shoves CARMELLE in front of a mug shot camera.*)

POLICEWOMAN. Shut up and move your ass. Here.

(*Hands CARMELLE a card with numbers on it. CARMELLE poses for a mug shot. The camera flashes.*)

POLICEWOMAN. Turn to your side.

(*CARMELLE does, poses again. Camera flash. POLICEWOMAN takes away card and pushes CARMELLE into a chair. Interrogation light comes up.*)

POLICEWOMAN. Sit down. (*Exits.*)

(*CARMELLE sits. VOICES from offstage interrogate her.*)

VOICE. (*Off:*) Why did you kill your friend Angelatina?
ANGELATINA. (*Off:*) Carmelle, you look lovely today.
VOICE. (*Off:*) You shot her, didn't you?
SINDEE. (*Off:*) Do it, Carmelle!
VOICE. (*Off:*) You blew her head off —
SINDEE. (*Off:*) Shoot her, you bitch —

PEPPER. (*Off.*) Sindee, stop it —
SINDEE. (*Off.*) I heard Brett fucked you —
VOICE. (*Off.*) Erased her face —
PEPPER. (*Off.*) Stop it!
SINDEE. (*Off.*) I heard you TOOK IT UP THE ASS!!!
CARMELLE. STOP IT!!!

(*LIGHTS SHIFT to courtroom. FEMALE JUDGE / LADY FOREWOMAN enters.*)

JUDGE. Lady Forewoman, have you reached a verdict in the case of Carmelle Constantine? (*Switches to FOREWOMAN.*) Yes, ma'am, we have. (*JUDGE*) And what is that verdict? (FOREWOMAN *reads:*) "In the case of Carmelle Constantine vs. the State of Illinois, we the jury find the defendant guilty of murder in the first degree."

(*The court CROWD can be heard reacting. JUDGE pounds her gavel for quiet.*)

JUDGE. In light of the heinousness of the crime of which you have been convicted, I hereby sentence you to be placed in a maximum-security juvenile detention center until the day of your eighteenth birthday, at which time you will be transferred to the Tubbville Penitentiary, where you will remain for the rest of your natural life.

(*FEMALE JUDGE bangs the gavel then exits as the CROWD cheers the verdict.*)

CARMELLE. No! I didn't do it! I didn't do it! I DIDN'T FUCK BRETT COOPER!!

(*POLICEWOMAN enters and drags CARMELLE off. SHIFT FOCUS TO –*)

Scene Fifteen

(*DENCH'S OFFICE. DENCH is doing paperwork. TERRI enters.*)

TERRI. Hello.
DENCH. Oh, hello.
TERRI. Um… I just wanted to stop by and apologize.
DENCH. For what?
TERRI. This. (*She opens a newspaper with the headline "Phys Ed Fem In Torrid Tangle With Pep Squad Sharp Shooter."*)

DENCH. (*Reads:*) "Phys Ed Fem In Torrid Tangle With Pep Squad Sharp Shooter." Why are you apologizing?

TERRI. My boss broke the story. Paula DeMarcato. "Pontificate With Paula."

DENCH. Oh. Well, you know it's not true.

TERRI. I know. Would it be so bad if it was?

DENCH. So you work in TV?

TERRI. Oh, yeah. With Paula. It bites, but my Dad owns the show. It'll be mine soon. She doesn't know it, but her neck's on the block.

DENCH. Really?

TERRI. Really.

DENCH. I always wanted to be in TV. Behind the scenes. Tellin' people what to do. That kind of stuff.

TERRI. Really? You know… I could take you on a tour. Of the studio.

DENCH. Yeah?

TERRI. Yeah! Any time.

DENCH. Yeah?

TERRI. Yeah.

DENCH. How about after school? Today.

TERRI. Sure! Sure, no problem.

DENCH. Are you hungry?

TERRI. Starved! I mean, yeah.

DENCH. How about having lunch on me. I mean, my treat.

TERRI. Sure. Where?

DENCH. School cafeteria. I get a discount.

TERRI. Do they have tater-tots today?

DENCH. They have tater-tots every day!

TERRI. I'm there!

(*They exit. SHIFT FOCUS TO –*)

Scene Sixteen

(*DETENTION CENTER. CARMELLE is tossed into her cell with BENNI, a tough female con who is lifting weights.*)

WARDEN'S VOICE. Get in there, you murdering lesbian psychopath!

BENNI. Ya got any cigarettes?

CARMELLE. Uh —

(*Before CARMELLE has a chance to answer, BENNI leaps up and beats the crap out of her in an extended fight scene. Then:*)

CARMELLE. Stop kicking my vagina!

BENNI. Listen up, honey! Things work different in the big dollhouse than on the outside. When I ask you for a butt, I don't want to hear any back talk, get it?

CARMELLE. Sure.

BENNI. Now gimme that butt!

CARMELLE. (*Presents her butt then realizes.*) Oh, you mean a cigarette. (*Hands Benni a cigarette.*)

BENNI. (*Snatches the entire pack.*) Thanks. It don't matter about your back-sassin' anyway, 'cause I ain't gonna be here much longer.

CARMELLE. You get out soon?

BENNI. Yeah, you could say that. See, some of us are goin' over the wall tonight.

CARMELLE. Oh… oh! You mean escape!

BENNI. Whew! Boy! I'm locked up with a Mensa scholar here!

CARMELLE. If I could get outta here, I could… Hey! Benni! Take me with you.

BENNI. What? You? Why should I? You're just a kid.

CARMELLE. Not anymore. I was a kid… twelve hours ago. But that twelve hours seems like twenty years after a strip search, a communal shower with fellow inmates with dubious intentions, and a meal of that swill they're passing off as food in the commissary. I'm a woman now. A woman of flesh and blood on the outside, with a stainless steel heart filled under pressure with piping hot bile that's ready to burst out and poison my body with its insidious disease. That disease is called revenge. And that disease has an antidote — Sindee Sandstone's head on a platter. And the only way I'm gonna cure what ails me is by gettin' outta the joint. So you gotta take me with ya. Ya gotta.

BENNI. Brilliant. Lovely. I'm cryin' inside. You gotta write that down, honey. You could be one of them romance writers for sure.

CARMELLE. So you'll take me with ya?

BENNI. Not a chance. You're too volatile. A real firecracker. We need someone with a cool head when the heat turns on. And cool you ain't.

CARMELLE. Oh, really? (*CARMELLE leaps on BENNI and beats her in an extended fight scene. She wrestles away the zip knife BENNI has and holds it to BENNI's throat.*)

BENNI. Okay! Okay, kid. Let's keep this calm.

CARMELLE. When do we move out?

BENNI. Midnight. Tonight.

CARMELLE. How?

BENNI. The cell door. It's unlocked. We paid one of the screws to get careless.

CARMELLE. Remember this little chat we had, Benni. If I feel somethin' sharp in my back on the way out, you can bet I'm gonna take a couple of you down with me when I go. Got it?

BENNI. Got it.

CARMELLE. Looks like it's time. Let's go.

(*They exit. SHIFT FOCUS TO –*)

Scene Seventeen

(*SINDEE'S BEDROOM. SINDEE is looking at herself in the mirror.*)

SINDEE. Yuck! (*She tries to make her face look thinner. She holds up a glamour magazine and compares.*) Sick! I'm so fucking fat!
CHARLENE. (*Off:*) Sindee! I don't hear that aerobics DVD!
SINDEE. Alright! Alright! Get off my back!
CHARLENE. (*Off:*) What?
SINDEE. Love you… bitch. (*She remains sitting at the mirror, examining herself.*) Gross. (*She plays with the flab under her arms and grimaces. She spies a bag of cookies. She looks at the flab, back at the cookies, back at the flab, back at the cookies, snatches up the cookies and crams one in her mouth.*)

(*Ghostly music plays.*)

SINDEE. What the fuck is that?

(*ANGELATINA enters as a ghost.*)

ANGELATINA. Hello, Sindee.
SINDEE. What the fuck?!
ANGELATINA. Yes, Sindee. It's me. Don't worry. Yes, I'm dead. You did your job.
SINDEE. My job? I didn't shoot you. I liked you. Carmelle shot you. She's bad. She's in jail right now.
ANGELATINA. Well, you got one out of three right. You didn't shoot me. But you sure didn't like me.
SINDEE. That's not true! I was jealous of you. I'll admit that. But you've got to understand. I'm a senior! It was my year! You know it's not right you're on the squad. You've got two more years left!
ANGELATINA. Not anymore. You took care of that.
SINDEE. I didn't shoot you! I told you! Carmelle shot you!
ANGELATINA. Then why do you have blood on your hands?
SINDEE. What? Do… oh, my God… what… it's… how?!
ANGELATINA. Goodbye for now, Sindee. Oh, and don't forget. One out of three.
SINDEE. What?!
ANGELATINA. You didn't shoot me. But you didn't like me, and Carmelle is not in jail.

SINDEE. She was booked today!

ANGELATINA. Watch your back. Don't get kicked where it counts.

SINDEE. Come back here!! Take this off my hands!!

(ANGELATINA disappears. SINDEE tries to wipe off her hands. CHARLENE, a bit drunk, enters with PEPPER. SINDEE hides her hands behind her back.

CHARLENE. Pepper is here.

PEPPER. Hi, Sin.

CHARLENE. Don't chitchat too long, girls. Sindee has swimnastics tomorrow before school.

SINDEE. Beat it, Mom.

CHARLENE. Excuse me, Miss Ma'am. Hey. What do you have behind your back?

SINDEE. Nothing. Get out!

CHARLENE. Let me see.

SINDEE. No.

CHARLENE. Let me see.

SINDEE. Mom, get out!

CHARLENE. You just don't want me to see because I want to.

SINDEE. And you just want to see because I don't want you to see. Get out!

CHARLENE. Come here! *(CHARLENE yanks SINDEE's hands out from behind her.)* There! Nothing? You were hiding nothing?

SINDEE. That's right. Now get out!

CHARLENE. Sometimes I know exactly why your father left. *(Exits.)*

PEPPER. What the hell was that?

SINDEE. Look at my hands!

PEPPER. So?

SINDEE. See anything?

PEPPER. No.

SINDEE. Carmelle escaped!

PEPPER. What?

SINDEE. Carmelle escaped. She's gonna kill me!

PEPPER. She's out? I just watched the news. They didn't mention it.

SINDEE. It's not on the news. Angelatina told me.

PEPPER. Shut up! Quit fucking around. We can't talk about it or we'll get caught.

SINDEE. But she did.

(Ghostly music plays. ANGELATINA enters.)

SINDEE. See! There she is! Can't you hear that?

PEPPER. What? Quit it, Sindee! Enough!

SINDEE. But... oh, I get it. Drive me crazy, right? So I'll do something stupid like turn myself in or fuck up. Well, it's not gonna work!

PEPPER. That's it! I'm outta here. I'm freaked out enough without you spazzing out on me. Bye! (*PEPPER exits.*)

SINDEE. Pepper, come back!

(*SINDEE exits after PEPPER. SHIFT FOCUS TO –*)

Scene Eighteen

(*ON THE ROAD. CARMELLE and BENNI flee.*)

CARMELLE. Move it!

BENNI. They're coming! I can hear them!

(*Sounds of dogs barking and police chase hubbub.*)

CARMELLE. You're slowing me up! Time to part ways, honey!

BENNI. Perfect. I don't want you taggin' along, anyway. I'm goin' this way.

CARMELLE. You ain't goin' anywhere! (*CARMELLE stabs BENNI, then puts the knife in BENNI's hands and pushes her off in the direction of the posse.*) I'll cut your hearts out!

(*The sound of guns killing BENNI. CARMELLE exits the opposite way. SHIFT FOCUS TO –*)

Scene Nineteen

(*OUTSIDE SINDEE'S HOUSE. SINDEE chases after PEPPER.*)

SINDEE. Pepper, get your ass back here!

PEPPER. Stuff it, Sindee! I can't take it anymore!

SINDEE. Can't take what anymore?

PEPPER. I'm going to the police!

SINDEE. Don't you dare!

PEPPER. I'm telling them everything! I can't live with this anymore!

(*CARMELLE steps out with a gun.*)

CARMELLE. Then you won't. (*She shoots PEPPER in the eye. PEPPER falls off stage, dead.*)

SINDEE. (*Suddenly happy:*) Carmelle! You're out! Hooray!

CARMELLE. Can it, Sandstone.

SINDEE. Okay. You're mad. I understand. I'd be mad to, if I'd been driven to the point of murder then set up to go to prison for the rest of my life.

But I think we both need to take a breath before we do something we might regret for the rest of our lives.

(*Ghost music plays. ANGELATINA appears.*)

SINDEE. Angelatina!
CARMELLE. Right.

(*ANGELATINA taps CARMELLE on the shoulder. CARMELLE turns and SINDEE wrestles the gun from her grip in an extended fight scene.*)

CARMELLE. Now Sindee, think about what you're about to do!
SINDEE. Okay.

(*SINDEE thinks for a moment, then shoots CARMELLE, who falls offstage, dead.*)

SINDEE. (*To Angelatina:*) Why did you help me?

(*Ghost music plays as ANGELATINA silently exits.*)

SINDEE. Come back! Augh! (*SINDEE wipes her hands on her skirt. Sirens sound.*) Shit! FuckpissSHIT!!

(*She exits. SHIFT FOCUS TO –*)

Scene Twenty

(*"PONTIFICATE WITH PAULA." Theme music plays. PAULA with CHARLENE and VERA. TERRI prompts the crowd with cue cards.*)

PAULA. Hello, everyone.
CROWD. Hello.
PAULA. How are you today?
CROWD. Fine, thanks.
PAULA. Today we've got two women. Very different women. Angry women. And you've already met one of them. Please welcome back Vera Vindechi. (*Applause.*) Hello, Vera.
VERA. Hello, Paula.
PAULA. Vera, you are very angry. And sad. Are you not?
VERA. Yes, I am.
PAULA. About?
VERA. About my daughter being murdered in cold blood. (*Cries.*)
PAULA. Our second guest is also angry. And sad. And a woman. Please meet Charlene Sandstone. (*Applause.*) Hello, Charlene.

CHARLENE. Hello, Paula. (*Waves to the cameras.*) Hi Ruby! Hi Kathy!

PAULA. Charlene, you've a heavy weight on your heart. Please unburden yourself for us.

CHARLENE. Well, apparently my daughter Sindee coerced one of her little friends to kill Vera's daughter then shot the rest of the cheerleading squad to death on our front lawn and is now running from the law. Kathy, look! Here's those shoes you let me borrow! (*Waves.*)

PAULA. Do you blame yourself?

CHARLENE. For what? That pudgy little psychopath? No sir. I blame her father, wherever that lazy son-of-a-bitch is. Bill, I hope you're proud, you idiot! Our daughter is on a killing spree!

PAULA. Vera, you must hate Charlene.

VERA. I don't hate anyone. I'm very angry with her. But I don't hate her.

PAULA. Do you think you could… forgive her?

VERA. As amazing as it may seem, I do think I can, someday, forgive her.

PAULA. I'm going to ask you two to do something right now. Something to start the healing. Do you think you could do something for me, Vera?

VERA. I'll try.

PAULA. Charlene?

VERA. (*Hasn't been paying attention:*) Huh? What? Oh… sure. Whatever.

PAULA. I want the two of you to give each other a hug. Okay?

(*CHARLENE reluctantly stands and allows VERA to hug her, a hug she does not return. VERA cries*)

PAULA. How about that, audience? Let's give them a hand. (*Applause.*) We're going to take a break —

(*WOMAN #2 with a gun stands up in the audience.*)

WOMAN #2. Everybody freeze!

TERRI. (*Under her breath:*) Just do it!

PAULA. What…?

TERRI. She's got a gun!

(*TERRI wrestles the gun away from WOMAN #2, who then flees out thru the audience into the lobby. TERRI gives chase. As PAULA, CHARLENE and VERA watch the offstage action, from the lobby we hear the gun go off once, then five more times. Theme music cuts in immediately after the last shot.*)

PAULA. We'll see you tomorrow on "Pontificate With Paula!" Bye!

VERA. She just fired a gun at you!

PAULA. Hmmm? Oh, yeah. Happens fairly regularly these days. Great show, girls.

CHARLENE. Thanks! You mean it? (*PAULA is already walking away.*) So, I guess you'll be dropping out of the contest.

VERA. Well...

PAULA. (*Whipping around.*) Contest? What contest?

VERA. Our coffee clatch has a little contest going to see who can grow the best garden. Whoever wins becomes the chairperson of the women's auxiliary. To answer your question, yes, I am going to keep going. I'm going to dedicate my plot to the memory of Angelatina.

CHARLENE. Eeeiw. Dead-icate is right. That's just plain morbid. Yuck!

PAULA. A garden contest? Sounds wonderful! I don't suppose you might need a celebrity judge?

VERA. Oh, would you? That would be wonderful! Especially since you and Angelatina had a special relationship, albeit a short one.

PAULA. Then it's settled. I'll be by when?

VERA. The end of the month.

PAULA. See you then. Bye! (*Exits.*)

VERA. Well, that brightened my spirits.

CHARLENE. Yes, I'm sure your daughter is thrilled. I gotta get out of here.

VERA. Oh, Charlene, did you drive?

CHARLENE. Yes. (*Exits.*)

VERA. Oh. Well, bye.

(*TERRI and MS. DENCH enter.*)

TERRI. And this is —

VERA. (*Startled:*) Oh!

TERRI. I'm sorry. Didn't mean to startle you.

VERA. That's okay.

DENCH. Terri is just giving me a tour of the studio.

VERA. How nice. By the way, the basketball wreath was quite lovely. You should be getting my thank-you card in the mail any day now. (*An awkward pause.*) Oh, how I go on. I'll leave you two girls to your own devices. Bye! (*Exits.*)

TERRI. So, this is the studio. This is where the magic happens. Well, more like voodoo if Paula is around.

DENCH. You don't like her much, do you?

TERRI. Hah!

DENCH. Why?

TERRI. Oh, I don't know. She's so weasely and... soft. Uck! I mean, get some balls already. Fend for yourself instead of having your lackeys do everything for you. See, I do my own hair and makeup, thank you.

DENCH. I can tell. It looks lovely. I don't know shit about makeup.

TERRI. Really? I could teach you. It's not hard.

DENCH. Really? Okay. Sure. Why not? It'll be fun!

TERRI. Yeah!

DENCH. What I really want you to teach me, though, is how to be on my own show.

TERRI. On TV?

DENCH. Sure! In college it was either Radio/TV broadcasting, or Phys Ed. It just seemed that the world of athletics had more to offer me at the time. But now I sort of regret spending all this time in the locker room. Sort of.

TERRI. Well, here. You sit down. I'll turn the camera on and you can look at yourself on the monitor. (*TERRI turns on camera.*)

DENCH. Wow. Hey, I'm on TV!

TERRI. Hey. I've got an idea. Let's go back to one of the small studios and tape some stuff. Just for fun.

DENCH. What kinda stuff?

TERRI. I'm sure we'll think of something. Come on.

(*They exit. SHIFT FOCUS TO –*)

Scene Twenty-One

(*GARDEN AREA. SINDEE sneaks on, with gun. She looks pretty bad, guzzling diet soda from a two-liter jug and stuffing cookies down her throat. She sees her mother's garden and flips it off. Ghost music plays. ANGELATINA appears.*)

SINDEE. That fucking music! Get the fuck away from me you zombie bitch! What do you want?! So you won't talk, is that it? Are those ghost rules? It that's what's happening now? Answer me!

(*ANGELATINA looks at CHARLENE's garden.*)

SINDEE. What?! It's my mother's garden. What?!! You want me to fuck up my mother's garden so your Mom can win that fucked-up contest? Is that it? Will that make you leave me the fuck alone? Huh? (*She goes over to the garden and stomps on it.*) There! Is that it? Huh? Is it?! ANSWER ME YOU FUCKING BITCH!!

(*ANGELATINA slowly turns away and exits. RUBY enters and sees SINDEE.*)

RUBY. Holy shit!

(*SINDEE flees.*)

RUBY. Police! Police! Police! Police! Police! Police!

(*The POLICEWOMAN finally enters.*)

RUBY. She went that way!

(*They exit off after SINDEE. SHIFT FOCUS TO –*)

Scene Twenty-Two

(*PAULA'S DRESSING ROOM. TERRI and DENCH enter.*)

TERRI. Come on, Paula, it's time to judge the contest.
PAULA. Alright, alright! What are you so excited about?
TERRI. You'll see. Come on! The cameras are already there.
PAULA. Alright, alright!

(*They exit. SHIFT FOCUS TO –*)

Scene Twenty-Three

(*GARDEN AREA. KATHY enters and does some last minute tending of her garden. CHARLENE enters.*)

KATHY. Hello, Charlene. Today's the big day.
CHARLENE. Was that a crack?
KATHY. What? No. The contest. The judging is in five minutes.
CHARLENE. Well, you can save it, Kathy, because you don't have a chance. And even if you win, nobody will stay in the Ladies Auxiliary if I tell them about what's really going on with Mr. Graham.
KATHY. You know, I was trying to tell someone something about you the other day, and they wouldn't believe me. And actually, they had me doubting it myself for a while. But I've come to realize my initial thought was right on the money.
CHARLENE. And what was that?
KATHY. You *are* full of shit! You're so full of shit, you're a health hazard to this and surrounding communities! You're so full of shit — you're not a Ziploc full of shit, you're not even a tall kitchen garbage bag full of shit. You're a drawstring, lawn and garden Hefty bag full of shit that's so packed full of shit you have to put it in another bag so it won't break open when you drag it to the dumpster! Screw you, Charlene Sandstone! You and that little murdering spawn of yours can rot in Hell for all I care! Go ahead and tell the world what happened to my husband! In fact, I'll save you the trouble! HEY! TUBBVILLE! KATHY GRAHAM'S HUSBAND LEFT HER! HE LEFT HER FOR ANOTHER MAN!

THEY LIVE IN FLORIDA AND OWN AN OFFICE SUPPLY STORE WITH THE HIGHEST RETAIL SALES IN THE HISTORY OF PAPER PRODUCTS! THEIR NET WORTH IS SEVEN FIGURES!! WHOOPEE!!

(*VERA, holding a photo collage of Angelatina, has entered during this.*)

VERA. Good afternoon, Kathy.

KATHY. Oh. Hello.

CHARLENE. What's that?

VERA. It's part of a shrine for Angelatina I'm going to include in my plot. It's beautiful, no?

CHARLENE. No. It's morbid and sick. Vera, you're just going to have to get over this whole thing and move on.

KATHY. Charlene! Her child was killed!

CHARLENE. It's been a week!

KATHY. She was killed by your daughter!

CHARLENE. Well, what would you like me to do about it? Apologize? I'm sorry! There! Does that make everything all better? No, of course not! So why should I have to say anything it if wasn't my fault and it won't repair a damn thing?

KATHY. Charlene!

VERA. Kathy, don't. It's alright. I've already forgiven her. I'm awfully thirsty. Would you girls like some tea?

KATHY. Yes, please. That would be very nice. (*Shooting CHARLENE a look:*) Charlene?

CHARLENE. Whoo, boy! Yes! Thirsty, thirsty, thirsty! I'd love some!

VERA. I'll be right back. (*Exits.*)

KATHY. You make me sick.

(*CHARLENE waves her off and goes over to her garden, which is trampled.*)

CHARLENE. What the hell...? Someone has ruined my garden! SOMEBODY HAS STOMPED UPON MY GARDEN! WHO DESTROYED MY GARDEN!!?? YOU DID IT, DIDN'T YOU?!

KATHY. I didn't touch your stupid garden!

CHARLENE. Where's Ruby? She was so jealous of my plot I bet she snuck over here in the middle of the night —

(*KATHY starts laughing.*)

CHARLENE. What are you laughing at?

KATHY. You!

CHARLENE. What?!

KATHY. (*Through convulsive laughter:*) You! Look at you stomping around. You look like a twelve-year-old with a broken toy! Hee hee hee! You look so petty... hee hee hee... you look so small! (*Gales of laughter.*)

CHARLENE. Shut your mouth!

(*VERA enters with tea.*)

VERA. Here it is. I'm sorry I don't have any NutraSweet —

CHARLENE. You!

VERA. Excuse me? What's so funny, Kathy?

CHARLENE. You did this to me! You destroyed my garden in some pathetic attempt to get revenge!

VERA. What are you talking about?

CHARLENE. You screwed up my chances to win in as payback because my little girl murdered your daughter. Don't look at me like that. I know your kind. Sweet on the outside but inside you're a festering sack of human waste just like the rest of us! Well it won't work this time, sister!

(*CHARLENE marches over to VERA's garden and stomps all over it. VERA and KATHY improvise horrified reactions.*)

KATHY. Charlene, stop!

(*PAULA, TERRI and DENCH burst in.*)

PAULA. It's judgment time!

VERA. It certainly is! Charlene Sandstone, I have put up with your whispering, your backstabbing, your snubs, crass comments and trash mouth, your racism, and the murder of my Angelatina by your promiscuous, eating-disordered, paranoid schizophrenic daughter. But you destroying my garden is the single meanest act I have ever had the misfortune to witness. I've wanted to say this to you for a long time, and here goes... I can't. I can't do it! And do you know why? Because I don't hate you, Charlene Sandstone. I pity you. And, in my mind, that's much worse. Good afternoon, everyone. (*Starts to leave then turns back.*) BITCH! I changed my mind. Boy, did that feel good! (*Exits.*)

PAULA. And we have a winner! Kathy Graham, congratulations! (*Puts blue ribbon on Kathy's garden.*)

KATHY. I won! I can't believe it!

(*SINDEE enters with gun.*)

SINDEE. Everybody freeze!

CHARLENE. Uh...Oh, Sindee! Thank goodness you're alive and well!

SINDEE. Shut up!

PAULA. Sindee Sandstone. Paula DeMarcato. I'd like to get your side of the story —

(*SINDEE shoots her dead. Theme music plays as she dies.*)

TERRI. And you're fired! My father saw Lila's audition tape and canned you!

SINDEE. Quiet!

KATHY. (*Quietly:*) Why'd you shoot Paula?

SINDEE. Because she started the whole thing with Angelatina being the queen and cheerleader.

DENCH. But I was the one who made her a cheerleader.

(*SINDEE shots DENCH.*)

SINDEE. Thank you so much. I'd totally forgotten that.

CHARLENE. Now, Sindee. Let's keep this in perspective. Why don't we go inside and have some pizza or something. You look hungry.

(*Ghost music plays. ANGELATINA enters.*)

SINDEE. (*To ANGELATINA.*) GET AWAY FROM ME!!

CHARLENE. Alright, I'm leaving.

SINDEE. Don't move! Seriously, does no one hear that?! (*To ANGELATINA.*) Why are you doing this to me? You got yourself into this mess, and now you're making me pay for it. It's not fair! You took my spot. My spot. I made it my spot. I had to! Because the old Sindee Sandstone was never pretty enough, was never talented enough, was never thin enough, was never good enough to be cheerleading captain. And I know this because that bitch right there told me every fucking day that I wasn't. She put me on a diet when I was eight years old. I was in aerobics at ten. Liposuction, collagen injections, foot binding, I've seen it all! And after all that, I am what you see before you today. Yes, I am talented. Yes, I am wizened. And yes, I am stunning. But at what cost? Angelatina paid. Pepper, Carmelle, they paid. Paula paid.

TERRI. What about Lila Dench?

SINDEE. Nah, I just hated her. I'm certainly going to pay. But do you know who hasn't paid? Hmmmm…?

(*KATHY takes a step away from CHARLENE, who gestures to TERRI.*)

SINDEE. No, mother. I don't know that woman. No.

(*CHARLENE points to KATHY.*)

SINDEE. No. Not Mrs. Graham.

(*CHARLENE points to TERRI again.*)

SINDEE. You! You haven't paid, mother! You!
CHARLENE. Oh, no. No, that's where you're wrong! I've paid! In spades! Look, someone has trampled my garden!
SINDEE. Okay, Mom — and I use that term loosely — time to pay up.
CHARLENE. Now, Sindee, stop it. Stop pointing that gun at me! You're scaring me!

SINDEE. Scaring you? Shit, lady — (*She shoots her mother dead.*) I'm killing you!

(*RUBY and the POLICEWOMAN burst in.*)

RUBY. There she is!
SINDEE. Come and get me, fuzz!

(*SINDEE races out with the POLICEWOMAN on her tail. TERRI moves over to LILA and tries to revive her.*)

KATHY. Ruby! Oh my goodness, Ruby!
RUBY. Hon, are you all right?
KATHY. I won! I won! I'm the new social chair! I won! I'm a winner! (*She flips CHARLENE's corpse the bird.*) Hooray for me!

(*POLICEWOMAN enter dragging SINDEE in cuffs.*)

SINDEE. Get your hands off me, pig! Ma, you look sick! Maybe you need a... shot! Ha ha hahahahaha... (*She is dragged off.*)
KATHY. Hooray! The witch is dead!

(*VERA rushes on holding a sheaf of papers.*)

VERA. What's going on?
RUBY. Didn't you hear? Sindee went on a killing spree then was captured by the police.
VERA. Gosh, no! I couldn't hear anything over the typewriter.
RUBY. Typing? What were you typing?
TERRI. She's alive! Hey! Lila Dench is alive!

(*LILA sits up weakly. BLACKOUT. In the black we hear a typewriter.*)

Scene Twenty-Four

(LIGHTS UP. TALK SHOW SET. Peppy, vaguely masculine theme music. DENCH is host. TERRI is floor manager.)

TERRI. And it's 5, 4, 3 —

(Two, one, on the air.)

DENCH. Pull up a chair and plant it, 'cause it's time for "Women!" The talk show for women, about women, and staffed entirely by women. *(Big applause.)* Today's guest is a woman, a survivor, and a sister of sorts. Please give a feminine, yet powerful, welcome to Vera Vindechi!

(Lots of applause. VERA enters looking great.)

VERA. Hello, Lila. It's nice to see you again.

DENCH. Thank you ever so. Now let's get down to brass tacks. You and I survived several months of Hell a short while back. And I took a bullet! *(Applause.)* Of course, I've got a talk show now, so that worked out well. But you, you've created something to expel all that pain and anger you felt, and now you're rakin' in a ton of cash. Ain't the U.S. of A grand? *(Applause.)*

VERA. It sure is!

DENCH. And here it is. *(Holds up the book.)* "My Dog Died, My Husband Left, My Other Dog Died, My Daughter Was Murdered *(Flips over the book, revealing the rest of the title on the back.)* And I'm Doin' Fine!"

VERA. And I am!

DENCH. We're going to talk about Vera's book, and the nightmare of losing her only child, plus her enchiladas suizas recipe that's sure to satisfy any lady tailgaters out there after the break. Stay with us, won't you?

(THEME MUSIC plays. Lights fade to black.)

END OF PLAY

A Pre-Condom Comedy by
Sean Abley

Adapted from the film L.A. TOOL & DIE by Joe Gage

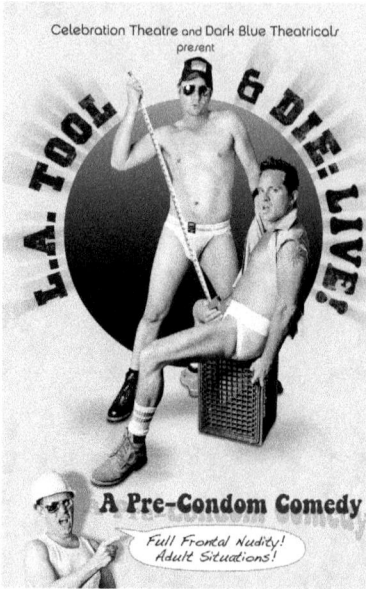

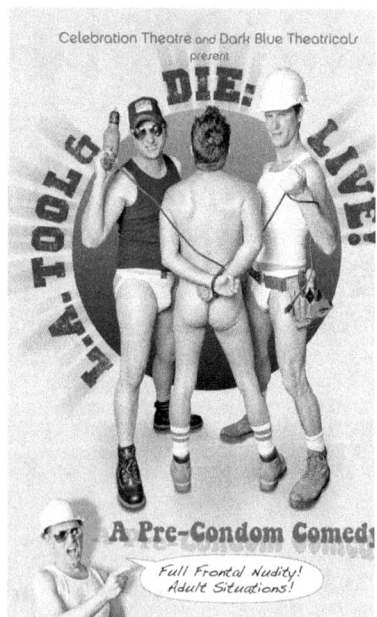

L.A. Tool & Die: Live! original postcard art, Celebration Theatre, Los Angeles 2010

<u>ACKNOWLEDGEMENTS</u>

L.A. Tool & Die: Live! was first performed at Celebration Theatre, West Hollywood CA, on July 30, 2010. Artistic Director, Michael Shepperd; Managing Director, Michael C. Kricfalusi. The production was directed by Sean Abley; produced by Sean Abley and Parnell D. Marcano; stage management by David Reynolds; lighting design by Matthew Brian Denman; scenic design by Robert Broadfoot; costume design by Rebecca Graves and Ben Kaufher; fight choreography by Kevin Held. The cast was as follows:

HANK	Thomas Colby-Dog
WILEY	Jon Gale
THE GAGE MEN	Paul A. Brown
	Tim Hearl
	Kevin Held
	James Jaeger
	Nathaniel Mathis
	Michael Vaccaro

Thomas Colby-Dog and Jon Gale, *L.A. Tool & Die: Live!*
Celebration Theatre, Los Angeles, 2010

CHARACTERS

HANK
JIM
VIC
HARRY
BARRY
WILEY
YOUNG KID
STRAIGHT MAN
GAS STATION ATTENDANT
WILEY'S DAD
COACH DAVIS
JACK
TANK
GABE

RAVEN
STRAIGHT WOMAN
FEMALE CLERK
CHARLENE

SAM, THE DOG – Played by a puppet in the original production, but could be played by a human in a costume.

THE DJs: RELIGIOUS NUT, SASSY BLACKWELL, COUNTRY WESTERN DJ, DR. LINDA, ARMED FORCES DJ, YUMA DJ, FEMALE EVANGELIST, EMERGENCY BROADCASTER

THE GAGE MEN

NOTE: All roles are to be played by men, including the female characters. The original production used an ensemble of eight actors.

PRODUCTION NOTES

Yes, some of the dialogue is terrible. Atrocious, even! But that's the fun of performing in a porn film on stage—porn acting! Also, there's a ton of what seem to be X-rated sex scenes in this script. Be creative! The original production managed to complete its multi-month, sold-out run without once being shut down due to obscenity charges. It can be done!

L.A. TOOL & DIE: LIVE!

By Sean Abley

Scene One

(*LIGHTS UP. HANK enters. He talks to the audience.*)

HANK. The name's Hank. You don't gotta know my last name. You just gotta know I'm a man who likes drinkin' beer, workin' hard, and playin' harder. I wear boots, unwashed jeans, and a shirt only when I have to. I work with my hands. I fix cars and trucks at the auto yard...that is, until they (*Take:*) shut down the yard. Things weren't the same after they (*Take:*) shut down the yard. But I got an invite for one last company meeting before they (*Take:*) tore the place down.

(*THE YARD. HANK enters to find JIM kneeling in front of GAGE MAN #1, who is lying across a table, pants down around his ankles. JIM is jacking the guy's cock. The other GAGE MEN stand around, watching. The scene is set up so JIM is facing upstage, so we don't actually see what is going on...but we can sure imagine...*)

JIM. Howdy, Hank. Thought I'd see you here today. Know how you used to love those company meetings.
HANK. Don't let me stop you. Looks like you got important business to discuss.
JIM. This guy's real hot. Just about ready to pop.

(*MUSIC CUE: 70's Porn Music. HANK and the GAGE MEN grope their crotches as they watch JIM blow and jack off GAGE MAN #1.*)

JIM / HANK / GAGE MEN. (*Cheering Gage Man #1 on:*) Yeah, fuck yeah! Fucking shoot that load! Spray that cum, buddy! Rhubarb, rhubarb, rhubarb! Peas and carrots, peas and carrots! etc.

(*GAGE MAN #1 orgasms, sending far too much cum flying thru the air.*)

JIM / HANK / GAGE MEN. Nice load, buddy! Fucking sweet load! etc.

(*GAGE MAN #1 gets up. He and the GAGE MEN move around the space. HANK approaches JIM and hands him a handkerchief to wipe off his face.*)

HANK. That was some good, masculine cock sucking. You're a masculine guy and I like that.

JIM. (*Suddenly girly:*) Thanks! (*Regains masculinity:*) I like your hairy chest and beard. Those rough edges get my dick hard.

HANK. I'm gonna miss these company meetings. Surprising how one auto scrap   yard could employ so many masculine cocksuckers. Guess if we sucked less
    cock and fixed more cars, we'd still be in business. Sad to see it go.

JIM. Fixin' to say 'So long' now that they (*Take:*) shut down the yard?

HANK. Guess so.

JIM. Got some time?

HANK. Nothing but now that they (*Take:*) shut down the yard.

JIM. Good. Why don't you take out that dick and let everyone see what it looks like.

(*HANK and the GAGE MEN all start unbuttoning their pants.*)

JIM. (*Thrilled:*) That's what I meant. Why don't all of you take out your dicks and let each other see what they look like.

(*HANK and the GAGE MEN all shove their pants down around their ankles,
leaving them naked from the waist down. MUSIC CUE: 70's Porn Music.*)

JIM. You want to beat off? Sure you do. Why don't you jack those dicks off until you cum in my face? You know that's what I like from those other times you did that, every day for the past month that this auto yard was open. When we got too horny from fixin' cars and doing other masculine things with our shirts off. And so I'd suck all your dicks and you'd jerk off on my face and then it would be quittin' time.

HANK. Okay men, let's circle the wagons.

(*HANK and the GAGE MEN all move toward JIM, who is now kneeling in the middle of the stage. With their pants around their ankles, they have to shuffle or hop across the stage - definitely more comedic than sexy.*)

JIM. Just what I like man. Workin' on this dick while you guys beat those fuckers... Didn't fix many cars, but made up for it in loads on my face...

GAGE MAN #2. Somebody shut this guy up already.

(*HANK and the GAGE MEN now surround JIM, who is unseen by the audience. They all jack their dicks as JIM, presumably, services them. JIM pokes his head out between the men for his lines.*)

JIM. I remember when Frank pulled that gasket out, ripped his shirt, took it off in a masculine, straight-acting way-- (*Trying to talk with a dick in his mouth sounds, then:*) --Jose took his uncut Mexican cock and slapped it on the counter-- (*Trying to talk with another dick in his mouth sounds, then:*) --that married guy with the tow truck driver-- (*Trying to talk with yet another dick in his mouth sounds, then:*) --and then it was quittin' time.

GAGE MAN #3. Fuck, I'm getting ready to shoot!

GAGE MAN #4. Yeah, I'm close!

JIM. Give it to me, man!

(*One by one, HANK and the GAGE MEN shoot their loads, with arcs of cum that hit the man across from them in the circle in the face.*)

ALL. (*Cheering each other on:*) Fuck yeah! I'm fucking cumming! Shoot that load, buddy! etc.

(*A beat, then all the men realize they have cum in their eyes and howl in pain.*)

ALL. (*In pain.*) My eyes! Fucking cum in my eyes! It burns!

(*The GAGE MEN peel off the circle and exit, rubbing their eyes. JIM stands up, unaffected, and hands HANK back his handkerchief.*)

JIM. (*re: the other men:*) Amateurs! So, you gonna hit the road now that they (*Take:*) shut down the yard?

HANK. Probably. Don't know yet. Might just hang out here for a bit.

JIM. We could hang out, man.

(*MUSIC CUE: 70's Porn Music.*)

JIM. Hang it all out. Work our dicks like we used to do when the auto yard was in full swing, and by swing I mean swingin' dicks shootin' their loads in my face--

HANK. I'm gonna go.

JIM. That's cool. Things aren't the same now that they (*Take:*) shut down the yard. Take it easy. (*Exits.*)

HANK. (*To audience:*) No work here, so gotta hit the road. But first a beer at this men's bar I go to.

Scene Two

(*HARRY'S OFFICE. HARRY sits at his desk doing the books. He calls his business partner, VIC, into the office.*)

HARRY. Vic, get in here!

VIC. Yeah, boss?

HARRY. I need you to go down to the men's bar and pick up a package.

VIC. The men's bar? That's a fag bar! What the fuck do I know about fag bars?

HARRY. You don't have to know nothing. All ya do is you go by a couple times a week and pick somethin' up. Do yourself a favor, Vic. This is the best thing we've ever bought into!

VIC. What am I, a fucking errand boy?

HARRY. Look, maybe you'll learn somethin'.

VIC. Shit...

HARRY. Vic, it's only for a coupla weeks, until I can get somebody regular.

VIC. I don't know, man...

HARRY. What do you think, it's catching? I been down to that bar every night for two weeks. In fact, I spent all Friday and Saturday night there, and look at me. Nothing. Do this as a favor to me, Vic...

VIC. Yeah, okay, sure...

HARRY. Now, you want to make sure you fit in. You can't go in looking like a straight guy or those queers will tear you apart.

VIC. What do I do?

HARRY. Ya gotta make like you're one of them. So first, ya gotta take off that shirt.

VIC. Take off my shirt?! What for?

HARRY. Ya gotta fit in, buddy. Those queers don't wear shirts if they can help it, even if it's below zero outside.

VIC. How do you... ?

HARRY. Ya hear things. Here, let me help.

VIC. Okay, fine. (*With Harry's help he takes off his shirt.*)

HARRY. You wearing underwear?

VIC. What?!

HARRY. You wearing drawers, bud? Them queers never wear underwear.

VIC. Why the fuck not?

HARRY. Takes too long for 'em to get to each others' rods. (*Off Vic's look.*) I read it in a magazine. If you're gonna fit in, ya better take off them drawers.

VIC. Here?

HARRY. What's the problem? We're both guys, right? It'll be just like a locker room. Lemme help ya...

VIC. I got it... (*He takes off his pants, takes off his underwear, then puts his pants back on.*) If you're shittin' me, Harry...

HARRY. (*Takes Vic's underwear and puts them in his pocket.*) There, now you'll fit right in. Get over there and pick up the package. Oh, and here, put this in your right back pocket. I see alot of 'em wearing these. (*Hands Vic a red handkerchief, which he puts in his right back pocket.*) There ya go. You'll have no problems now, Vic.

VIC. You sure know a lot about them fags, Harry.

HARRY. It was on the "Donahue," they did a whole hour on them fudgepackers and their... fudgepackery. Now get the fuck over there and get that package!

VIC. Alright, alright.

(*VIC exits. HARRY pulls out Vic's underwear.*)

HARRY. They're gonna love ya! (*A beat. Another guilty beat. Then finally...Harry puts the underwear to his nose and inhales. He exits.*) Ah, yeah!

Scene Three

(*THE BAR. MUSIC UP. The GAGE MEN, WILEY and BARRY enter. BARRY [who wears super short jean cutoffs] talks a mile a minute, while WILEY tries to jump in and/or scopes out other guys in the bar.*)

BARRY. (*Nonstop:*) I like your look, man. That cowboy hat knocks me out. Looks like you shrunk those 501s in the bathtub, make 'em skintight. You ever do that? You know sometimes I'll shrink my 501s in the bathtub, just sit in the hot water, then dry 'em, then toss 'em in the washer again with a little bleach to wear 'em out, then dry 'em, then put 'em on and take a, what are those things? Not a file...a rasp! Yeah, take a rasp and right over my package I'll sort of file it down...funny I'm saying "file" but I'm using a rasp. Anyway, I file it down just a little, so the part over my cock is a little lighter, so it makes it look like my cock is so big it's wearing out my jeans. My cock is pretty big, by the way.

(*LIGHT SHIFT - BAR SPOT. HANK and VIC enter the bar from different parts of the stage and bump shoulders as they cross, edging past each other, as if it's very crowded in the bar.*)

HANK. Excuse me.

VIC. Watch it!

HANK. Just gotta get by. Bar's packed tighter than sardines.

VIC. Just watch it.

(*HANK and VIC comically run their hands over each others' bodies as they pass each other in the "crowded" bar.*)

HANK. Sorry, man, crowded.

VIC. Back up!

HANK. Just gotta get by ya...

VIC. Fuck, move over!

HANK. Almost there, sorry buddy...

VIC. Cut the shit, man!

(*HANK and VIC finally separate. VIC exits. HANK crosses to the other side of the bar, where he and WILEY's eyes meet. ALL freeze except HANK and WILEY. LIGHT SHIFT. MUSIC CUE: Romantic Music. LIGHT SHIFT back to FULL BAR.*)

BARRY. (*Talking about his shorts:*) ...and then I cut them up above the pockets, but left the pockets hanging, so you can see my jockstrap in the back, and if you look close, my package in front. Man, I fucking love these shorts! Cut off jeans are never gonna go out of style!

(*WILEY [ignoring BARRY] and HANK lock eyes. ALL freeze except HANK and WILEY. LIGHT SHIFT. MUSIC CUE: Romantic Music. LIGHT SHIFT back to FULL BAR.*)

BARRY. When you're a masculine guy like me-- (*Reacting to the music:*) Holyshitthisismysong! (*Starts dancing around Wiley and singing.*) Ring my bell! Ding dong ding, aahhhhh ahhhh! Ring it!

(*WILEY is shyly smiling at HANK, who is cruising him hardcore. HANK puts the wrong end of a cigarette in his mouth. A GAGE MAN reaches over, takes it out, and turns it around for him. HANK gives him a "Thanks" nod, then goes back to eyeing WILEY.*)

BARRY. Ring my bell! Man, this is a classic! The girl who sings this? Anita Ward? She's gonna have a long career, my friend.

(*HANK motions for WILEY to come over. WILEY hesitates, then shakes his head "No." MUSIC changes to "YMCA."*)

BARRY. (*Stops dancing.*) Jesus, really? I hate this song. Is anybody really gonna remember "YMCA" thirty years from now?
WILEY. I gotta go. Nice meeting you. (*He moves to exit.*)

(*WILEY and HANK meet center. ALL freeze except HANK and WILEY. LIGHT CHANGE. MUSIC CUE: Romantic Music. HANK takes the lit cigarette out of his mouth and puts it in the hand of a frozen GAGE MAN. HANK and WILEY almost kiss, then HANK freezes as WILEY talks to the audience.*)

WILEY. (*To audience:*) I just fell in love with a guy who I've never spoken to or seen before. But it's real. I know it is. And that's why I have to leave and never see him again. (*Exits.*)

(*LIGHT CHANGE to FULL BAR. MUSIC up. Action unfreezes. GAGE MAN reacts to a lit cigarette in his hand. HANK is confused - where is WILEY? BARRY dances over to HANK.*)

HANK. Tough luck, amigo.
BARRY. Man, that guy drives me crazy. He can really fill out a pair of jeans.
HANK. Fuck, man.
BARRY. He kept looking at you.
HANK. I know.
BARRY. And he didn't even talk. And I'm a great conversationalist. You want to talk about my dancing? (*Dances in front of Hank.*)
HANK. Sure. (*Pushes Barry aside by the face, then crosses the stage.*)

(*LIGHT SHIFT - BAR SPOT. HANK crosses the stage, meeting VIC in the middle again. Their hands are all over each other as they try to pass in the "crowded" bar.*)

HANK. Wanna dance?
VIC. Jesus, they do that here, too? Jesus!
HANK. Jesus? I think he's giving head in the pisser.
VIC. Don't take the Lord's name in vain!
HANK. I think you're in the wrong place buddy.
VIC. You said it! (*Exits.*)
HANK. I gotta get some air. (*Exits.*)

Scene Four

(*PARKING LOT. MUSIC (Country) from the radio. WILEY is sitting in his van with his dog, SAM.*)

WILEY. Dammit, Wiley, drive away! Why are you sitting here in this parking lot?
SAM. Arf! Arf!
WILEY. It ain't like that, Sam. I can't be messin' with just any Tom, Dick or Harry with a fuckable ass, chiseled chest and a mustache that would look good wrapped around my dick that crosses my path. It wouldn't be right.
SAM. Arf! Arft! Arf!
WILEY. I don't care what I promised Jack! That has nothin' to do with it!
SAM. Arf! Arf! Arf!
WILEY. You take that back!
SAM. Arf!
WILEY. You shut your mouth!

(*HANK enters and walks over to WILEY in the van.*)

HANK. First time I heard that from a cowboy.
WILEY. Oh, hi.
HANK. Hello, cowpoke. And who's this? (*Pets Sam.*)

WILEY. That's my buddy Sam.

HANK. Good doggie...

WILEY. (*Notices Sam's little doggy dick poking out.*) Sam! You put that away! Sorry. That always comes out when you scratch him down there.

HANK. And what happens if I scratch you down there?

WILEY. I really shouldn't have been in there.

HANK. Yeah? (*Touches Wiley's face, runs his fingers over his cheeks.*)

WILEY. Yeah. I really should be going.

HANK. You sure about that? (*Sticks his fingers in Wiley's mouth.*)

WILEY. You know, you're okay. In fact, I mean you're really... I just... I don't think I'm into sport fucking.

HANK. I get ya. Maybe another time.

WILEY. I can't. I'm gotta leave for L.A. I got a job waiting. You know how it is.

HANK. (*Crushed, but manly.*) Sure.

WILEY. See ya.

HANK. So long. (*Wiley freezes as he crosses away. To the audience:*) That was the big one. Sure was. Sure as Hell was! And I didn't even get his fucking name! (*Cries like a woman as he exits.*)

WILEY. (*Unfreezes.*) You're a fool! You're damn fool, Wiley!

SAM. Arf!

WILEY. Can't turn back now, Sam. I got a job waitin' in Los Angeles. L.A., here we come! (*They exit.*)

Scene Five

(*BAR BATHROOM. The GAGE MEN and BARRY crowd in around the trough, pissing at the same time. VIC enters.*)

VIC. Move over, I gotta piss.

(*VIC steps up to the trough, unzips and pulls out his dick to piss. The GAGE MEN and BARRY all shoot each other looks, then immediately move in closer alongside VIC, making no secret that they're looking at VIC's dick.*)

VIC. Hey! Stop looking at my big, fat, straight cock!

(*A GAGE MAN pops up from the trough.*)

GAGE MAN. (*Spits.*) Asparagus!

(*HANK enters. He wedges his way in front of the trough next to VIC, unzips and starts to piss.*)

VIC. Oh, great.

HANK. (*Notices the red hanky in Vic's right pocket.*) Red hanky right, huh? Didn't figure you for the type. Well, the boys and I can help ya with that. Come on, boys!

ALL. Whoo hoo! Yeah! etc.

GAGE MAN. There's gonna be a fistin'!

(*HANK, BARRY and the GAGE MEN grab VIC and strip off his pants. They hold him in a fisting bottom position. Suddenly someone has rubber gloves, and someone else produces a can of Crisco. VIC struggles but can't get free.*)

VIC. Wait! What are you doing?

HANK. We're gonna give you a hand, brother. (*Smacks Vic's butt.*) Right up the ol' fudge tunnel.

VIC. What?! (*Sees the Crisco.*) Crisco?!

GAGE MAN. (*Commercial spokesperson:*) It's butter flavored!

VIC. Get the fuck off me!

HANK. What are you afraid of? We're just going to stick our hands up your ass.

GAGE MEN. (*Clapping.*) Yay!

VIC. Stop!

HANK. Your lips say, "No," but your ass says, "Open all night!"

VIC. You fucking faggots!

ALL. (*Back away, hands off.*) Ooooohhh.....

HANK. Fistin's over boys.

GAGE MEN. Awwww... (*They exit back to the bar.*)

VIC. Look, asshole, you and me got a problem. I don't take kindly to you and your fruity friends taking liberties with my backside.

HANK. So what's it gonna be, we gonna duke it out or what?

VIC. Cocksucker...

HANK. You better believe it. If there's anything I like better than sucking cock, it's kicking ass!

(*A BOXING MATCH BELL rings. All the GAGE MEN enter as spectators, cheering the two men on. HANK strips off his shirt, and the two men begin to fight. HANK get's the better of VIC very quickly, eventually landing some punches that knock VIC to the floor. END OF ROUND BELL rings. A GAGE MAN comes out, a la a ring girl, in a jockstrap, carrying a sign that reads "Round 2".*)

VIC. You crazy fuck!

HANK. (*Mocking him:*) You lunk head!

VIC. You asshole!

HANK. (*Mocking:*) You pork chop!

GAGE MEN. Ooooohhh....

(ROUND TWO BELL rings. VIC tries to get to his feet, but HANK will have none of that.)

HANK. Oh, no you don't.

(HANK pummels VIC a few more times. VIC finally backs away.)

HANK. Tired of gettin' your ass kicked by a faggot?
VIC. *(Hissy fit:)* Shut up! Just shut up! *(Exits.)*

(EVERYONE laughs at VIC as he skitters away. The GAGE MEN disperse. BARRY approaches HANK, who has become contemplative.)

HANK. That jasper sure thought he was a mean cuss, huh...?
BARRY. You okay?
HANK. Sure. Nothing like a punch out to clear the head. *(Suddenly cries like a woman.)*
BARRY. Aw, you still thinking about that guy Wiley?
HANK. Is that his name?
BARRY. Yeah.
HANK. First or last?
BARRY. Don't know. Just Wiley...
HANK. Did he tell you where he was going?
BARRY. Yeah, he said he was going out west to someplace called L.A. dot dot dot...
HANK. Yeah?
BARRY. L.A. ellipses...
HANK. Yeah?!
BARRY. L.A. Tool and Die!

(MUSIC CUE: Theme Music. HANK moves to leave.)

BARRY. Where ya goin'?
HANK. *(To the audience:)* I'm goin' to drive a thousand miles across the country to find the man I love. I'm going to find, uh...
BARRY. Wiley.
HANK. Wiley!

(HANK exits, leaving BARRY dancing on stage. HANK returns, pushes BARRY off by the face, then exits again.)

Scene Six

(ON THE ROAD IN WILEY'S VAN. WILEY and SAM listen to the radio as they drive. LIGHTS UP ON RADIO STATION. A RELIGIOUS NUT talks into his microphone.)

RELIGIOUS NUT. You know, I think Jesus has a sense of humor. I really do. Now take the Vietnam War. Now there's a chuckle for ya. I don't mind sayin' I think we should get rid of gooks, cuz gooks don't believe in Jesus. They don't! They believe in Buddha. Anybody believe in Buddha, I don't have nothing to do with them! If you can't believe in Jesus - fuck ya! I'm sorry, what I meant to say was - fuck your mother and all her people!

(*WILEY changes the channel on the radio. The RELIGIOUS NUT changes voices and costume pieces onstage and immediately becomes female soul DJ, SASSY BLACKWELL .*)

SASSY BLACKWELL. It's nighttime, ladies and gentlemen. It's time for Dark Grooves with your lady of the night, Sassy Blackwell. First up, [NAME OF SONG].

(*MUSIC CUE: Radio song. WILEY spots RAVEN walking down the highway.*)

WILEY. Look, Sam, a girl walking down the highway! Should we pick her up?
SAM. Arf! Arf!
WILEY. But she looks like she needs help. I'm pulling over.

(*WILEY pulls over and sticks his head out the window.*)

WILEY. Need a lift?
RAVEN. No, that's okay. I don't have far to go.
WILEY. Pretty deserted out here.
RAVEN. Don't you worry about me, I can take care of myself. (*A beat. Angrily:*) Go on! I'm alright. Honest.
WILEY. Well, okay...
RAVEN. Drive safely. (*Moves away from the van.*)
WILEY. I wonder what she's up to...
SAM. Arf!

(*WILEY shrugs and drives away. Another car approaches driven by FRED. RAVEN instantly sticks her thumb out, hitchhiker style. FRED pulls over and leans out his window.*)

FRED. Do you need some help?
RAVEN. (*Suddenly using a French accent:*) Oh, yes! I am lost in your country, and my car is broken, and I am French!
FRED. How horrible! Please, get in. I'll take you to the next town.
RAVEN. (*French.*) Merci beaupooh.

(*RAVEN gets in the car. They drive down the road.*)

FRED. My name's Fred. What's yours?

RAVEN. Raven.

FRED. "Raven". That's really unusual, isn't it?

RAVEN. Mmm hmmm.

FRED. I took a little French in high school.

RAVEN. (*Drops accent:*) Really? (*French.*) Oh, oui?

FRED. Bonjour, mon nom est Fred. Bonjour, mon nom est Fred. Vous ?es tr? joli. Quel est votre nom? (*Hello, my name is Fred. You are very pretty. What is your name?*)

RAVEN. (*French.*) Uh, Jean Nate, croissant, Channel Number Five.

FRED. Huh, my French must be a bit rusty.

RAVEN. (*French.*) Nice car.

FRED. Thanks! Just got it yesterday.

RAVEN. (*French.*) Too bad.

FRED. Too bad? I don't understand...

RAVEN. You just got it yesterday, (*Drops accent.*) and you lost it today. (*Pulls out a gun.*)

FRED. Oh, I don't believe this...

RAVEN. Believe it. Pull over there.

FRED. If it's money you want...

RAVEN. Get out!

(*FRED and RAVEN get out of the car. She indicates with the gun for him to move to a nearby tree.*)

RAVEN. Over there. Here. (*Hands him a pair of handcuffs.*)

FRED. Oh no, come on...

RAVEN. Put 'em on. First one hand. Now put your arms around this tree and lock them.

(*FRED locks his hands around the tree.*)

RAVEN. Later, alligator! Have a nice life! (*Gets in the car and drives away.*)

FRED. Help! Help! Is there anybody out there?

(*MUSIC: Horror Movie underscore. A STRANGER, wearing a ski mask and carrying a knife, appears in the shadows. He puts a stick on the ground, then steps on it, causing it to audibly snap.*)

FRED. (*Hears the snap.*) Who's there? Hey you, in the ski mask, carrying the knife. Hey, can you help me? Do you have any bolt cutters?

(*The STRANGER slowly approaches FRED from behind. He reaches around FRED and undoes his pants, then pulls them down around his ankles.*)

FRED. Uh, hi. Nice to meet you. Look, maybe you could use that knife to jimmy the cuffs? Or do you have a hairpin or something? I mean, no offense, but you could have anything under that ski mask...

(*The STRANGER grabs the waistband of FRED's underwear, pulls it out, then uses his knife to cut thru the fabric. He cuts FRED's underwear off and tosses them aside.*)

FRED. Are you kidding? First my new car, now my underwear? Could this day get any (*Sticks butt out.*) worse?

(*The STRANGER unzips his pants with a big SFX "Zzzzzip!" The STRANGER positions himself behind FRED and mounts him. He fucks a very vocal FRED roughly*)

FRED. Wait... Hey! (*With each thrust, should sound like cries for help at first:*) Eee! Iiii! Oh! You!

STRANGER. And some times why! Why! Why! (*Sudden change.*) Why do you insist I wear this ski mask? I'm basting in this thing.

FRED. It makes me horny for you, baby.

(*STRANGER pulls out, puts it back in his pants and zips up. He walks around FRED to the handcuffs, which he unlocks with a key from his pocket.*)

FRED. Thank you. Those handcuffs were chafing my wrists.

STRANGER. (*Takes off his mask.*) Raven wanted an extra ten bucks.

FRED. Why?

STRANGER. Said it's getting dangerous out here. Some guy tried to pick her up.

FRED. So, next time we'll give her real bullets.

STRANGER. You want to go back to the house?

FRED. No, let's go grab something to eat. All that raping makes me starving. You buy - you owe me for the underwear.

(*FRED and STRANGER exit.*)

Scene Seven

(*ONE THE ROAD IN HANK'S TRUCK. HANK is driving down the road listening to the radio. LIGHTS UP ON RADIO STATION. A COUNTRY WESTERN DJ talks to his listeners.*)

COUNTRY WESTERN DJ. That was "Cryin' In My Beer, Then Drinkin' My Tear-filled Beer, Cuz I Don't Wanna Waste a Good Beer Over You" by Gator Davis. Next up, "My Baby Left Me for a Truck".

(*HANK switches off the radio.*)

HANK. (*Wipes away tears.*) Damn you, Wiley! You got me cryin' over bad country western music.
WILEY V.O. You shut your mouth!

(*FLASHBACK LIGHTS and MUSIC. WILEY enters in his van. HANK gets out of the truck. We hear the conversation between WILEY and HANK. HANK lip syncs along perfectly, while WILEY just moves his mouth during his dialogue, obviously not matching.*)

HANK. (*Flashback lip sync:*) First time I heard that from a cowboy.
WILEY. (*Flashback bad lip sync:*) Oh, hi.
HANK. (*Flashback lip sync:*) What's happening?
WILEY. (*Flashback bad lip sync:*) I really shouldn't have been in there.
HANK. (*Flashback lip sync:*) Yeah? (*Touches Wiley's face.*)
WILEY. (*Flashback bad lip sync:*) Yeah. I really should be going.
HANK. (*Flashback lip sync:*) You sure about that? (*Puts his fingers in Wiley's mouth.*)
WILEY. (*Flashback bad lip sync:*) You know, you're okay. In fact, I mean you're really... I just... I don't think I'm into sport fucking.
HANK. (*Flashback lip sync:*) I get ya. Maybe another time.
WILEY. (*Flashback bad lip sync:*) I'm leaving for L.A. in the morning. I got a job waiting. You know how it is.
HANK. (*Flashback lip sync:*) Sure.
WILEY. (*Flashback bad lip sync:*) See ya. (*Exits.*)

(*LIGHTS RESTORE. MUSIC OUT. WILEY exits. HANK is now standing alone outside his truck. SFX: TRUCK DRIVING ON ITS OWN. HANK realizes he's out of his truck [which is still running], panics and races back to his truck, which is barreling down the road.*)

HANK. Whoa! (*Jumps in his truck.*) That boy's got me tied up in knots!

(*A sign, "Swimmin' Hole," pops out.*)

HANK. Swimmin' hole? Man, I need a good bath. Been stuck in this truck with just my thoughts for too long.

(*SWIMMING HOLE. HANK pulls his truck over and gets out. He pulls off his shirt and gets ready to get into the water. He hears a sound and quickly hides. A YOUNG KID, wearing a backpack, sneaks up, hiding in the bushes. Unaware of HANK, he takes out a porn mag, flipping thru the pages with one hand, the other in his pants. After a moment a STRAIGHT*)

COUPLE *drive up. The YOUNG KID and HANK both keep hidden, watching the couple.*)

STRAIGHT WOMAN. What are you pulling over for?

STRAIGHT MAN. I'm so horny for you baby, I gotta pull over and take care of business!

STRAIGHT WOMAN. Take care of what business?

STRAIGHT MAN. Your pussy business! Come on!

STRAIGHT WOMAN. If you think for one minute I'm going to fuck you at this swimming hole-- (*Holds up her panties.*) Oh, look, my panties flew off! My vagina is possessed! It has a mind of it's own!

STRAIGHT MAN. Yes!

(*STRAIGHT MAN jumps on STRAIGHT WOMAN and they have fast, furious, out of control sex. HANK and the YOUNG KID masturbate as they watch.*)

STRAIGHT MAN. I'm putting on a condom because I don't want to get you pregnant! (*Puts on a condom, then mounts her.*) Missionary!

STRAIGHT WOMAN. Oh, God, yes! Right there! Keep doing that! More of that! Harder! Faster! Don't touch my hair!

STRAIGHT MAN. Oral! (*Change positions.*) Yeah, baby, suck that dick! Take it! I'm giving it to you, now you take it! Suck that cock! Do what I tell you! Suck it!

STRAIGHT WOMAN. Don't touch my hair!

STRAIGHT MAN. Doggy style! (*Change positions.*)

STRAIGHT WOMAN. Yes! More! Take it! Punch that pussy! Punch that pussy! Punch it like a time card that you punch for your job of fucking me! Keeping fucking me! Overtime! Overtime!

STRAIGHT MAN. Reverse cowgirl! (*Change positions.*)

STRAIGHT WOMAN. I'll be your cowgirl! Giddyup! Yes! Whoo hoo! Ride 'em cowgirl!

STRAIGHT MAN. (*Orgasms:*) Oh, God, I'm cumming! I"m cumming!

STRAIGHT WOMAN. (*Orgasms:*) Don't touch my hair!!

(*The STRAIGHT COUPLE finishes.*)

STRAIGHT WOMAN. Oh, that was so good! That was better than the last three times you fucked me senseless in the car this morning! I love you -

STRAIGHT MAN. Get off me! Let's go!

(*The YOUNG KID makes a noise and the STRAIGHT COUPLE notices him.*)

STRAIGHT MAN. Looks like we have an audience.

STRAIGHT WOMAN. Did that kid see us? Oh, my God, my hair...

(*The STRAIGHT MAN takes off the used condom and throws it to the YOUNG KID.*)

STRAIGHT MAN. There ya go, kid!

(*The STRAIGHT COUPLE gets back in their car and drives away. The YOUNG KID snatches up the used condom and shoves it in his bag. HANK reveals himself to the YOUNG KID.*)

HANK. Now don't you go wastin' that. That's good eatin'!

(*The YOUNG KID takes off. HANK busts out laughing.*)

Scene Eight

(*GAS STATION. WILEY pulls up in his truck to the pumps. We hear the radio. LIGHTS UP ON RADIO STATION. DR. LINDA giving advice to a CALLER, who is also onstage with a phone.*)

DR. LINDA. Okay, next caller. You're on with Dr. Linda. What's your problem?
CALLER. Well, I've been having...feelings...for my coworker. My male coworker. And I'm not sure what to do about it.
DR. LINDA. Do about it? There's nothing to do about it but enjoy it! Enjoy all the kissing, the five o'clock shadow brushing against your cheek, exploring each other nipples, mounting each other in the rectum. Enjoy it all, because come judgment day you'll be burning in a lake of fire. Next caller!

(*WILEY clicks off the radio. The GAS STATION ATTENDANT walks up.*)

GAS STATION ATTENDANT. (*Grabbing his crotch suggestively.*) Fill 'er up?
WILEY. (*Not noticing.*) Yeah, please. Unleaded.
GAS STATION ATTENDANT. Oh...gas. (*Picks up gas nozzle and moves to the gas tank.*) I think I remember how to use this thing... (*Grabs his crotch as he fills the tank.*)
SAM. Arf! Arf!
WILEY. What? No, he did not. He'd lose his job for that! Don't be silly.
SAM. Arf!
WILEY. You shut your mouth!

(*FLASHBACK LIGHTS and MUSIC. HANK enters. Much like before, but reversed. WILEY lip syncs perfectly, while HANK just moves his mouth.*

Maybe smokes a cigarette while he's supposed to be talking? You get the idea....The lines are faster this time.)

HANK. (*Flashback bad lip sync:*) First time I heard that from a cowboy.
WILEY. (*Flashback lip sync:*) I really shouldn't have been in there.
HANK. (*Flashback bad lip sync:*) You sure about that? (*Sticks his fingers in Wiley's mouth.*)
WILEY. (*Flashback lip sync:*) I'm leaving for L.A. in the morning. I got a job waiting. You know how it is.
HANK. (*Flashback bad lip sync:*) Sure.
WILEY. (*Flashback lip sync:*) See ya.

(*HANK exits. LIGHTS RESTORE. MUSIC OUT.*)

WILEY. Hey, you got a restroom?
GAS STATION ATTENDANT. Yeah, out back.
WILEY. Thanks.
GAS STATION ATTENDANT. (*Hand on his crotch.*) Take your time. No one using it this time of day.
SAM. Arf!
WILEY. Shush! He is not!
GAS STATION ATTENDANT. Key's on the hook by the door.

(*RESTROOM. There is a gloryhole in the wall. WILEY enters and unzips. OUTSIDE THE RESTROOM the GAS STATION ATTENDANT positions himself [unseen to the audience] by the gloryhole. He motions to WILEY thru the hole.*)

WILEY. What the…? (*Considers it for a moment as the GAS STATION ATTENDANT puts his mouth up to the hole.*)
WILEY'S BRAIN V.O.. I just...I don't think I"m into sport fucking....
WILEY'S MOM'S VOICE V.O. If you touch your....down there...you'll go blind...
IRISH PRIEST'S VOICE V.O. Remember, every time you think unclean thoughts or touch your penis, an angel dies...
WILEY. Shut up, brain!
WILEY'S BRAIN V.O. Okay...

(*WILEY hesitates, then stands and jams his cock thru the hole.*)

GAS STATION ATTENDANT. Augh! My eye! Slow down!
WILEY. Oh, sorry. I'll take it slow.

(*WILEY pauses for a beat, then jams his cock back into the gloryhole and pounds way for a comically vigorous blowjob from the GAS STATION ATTENDANT. WILEY cums, and we hear the GAS STATION ATTENDANT...*)

GAS STATION ATTENDANT. Aaaaaugh!
WILEY. (*Bends down to talk thru the gloryhole.*) Thank you!

(*WILEY exits the BATHROOM and goes back to his van.*)

SAM. Arf!
WILEY. None of your business!

(*WILEY drives away as HANK arrives in his truck. The GAS STATION ATTENDANT approaches the car.*)

GAS STATION ATTENDANT. Fill 'er up?
HANK. I'm looking for a guy who mighta come thru here. Cowboy type, blond, beard, maybe talkin' to his dog? I gotta find him.
GAS STATION ATTENDANT. (*Turns to reveal he is now wearing an eye patch.*) He poked out my eye with his cock in my restroom gloryhole.
HANK. I'm gonna marry that guy. Thanks buddy!

Scene Nine

(*ON THE ROAD IN WILEY'S VAN. WILEY drives as he and SAM listen to the radio. LIGHTS UP ON RADIO STATION. ARMED FORCES DJ broadcasts to his listeners.*)

ARMED FORCES DJ. Alright, that was Beverly Sills and Kenny Rogers singing together at the USO show in Brussels last Fall. Didn't realize there were lyrics to the "Theme from 'Star Wars'", but there you have it. And now back to the serious news, people. Events in the Middle East, it says here, continue to escalate into a crisis situation not seen since our involvement in Southeast Asia....
WILEY. We're near Yuma, Sam. That's where I grew up. Wonder what's on the local radio. (*Switches the radio station.*)

(*RADIO STATION. ARMED FORCES DJ becomes pot-smoking YUMA DJ broadcasting to his listeners.*)

YUMA DJ. (*Takes a big hit.*) I just got back from a great trip to Sedona. Got some great turquoise jewelry from the indigenous tribes, dug some amazing crystals, and picked up some tax-free cigarettes from the reservation. But enough about me. What's going on in Yuma this weekend? Yuma High School will be hosting the Tuscon High Badgers in the cross-state regional football game. The Yuma Pumas are coached by head coach Earl Davis, who retires this year...

WILEY. Coach Davis! Man, I haven't thought about him in years. Sam, I remember when I was on the football team, and I couldn't get Coach Davis to move me up to varsity. He even called my dad in for a meeting to talk about it. I wonder what he said to him...

(*COACH DAVIS'S OFFICE, 1969. There should be a desk and one chair. COACH DAVIS and WILEY'S DAD enter.*)

WILEY'S DAD. Coach, I'm telling you, if you'd just give my kid a chance...
COACH DAVIS. Mr. Carson, I'd like to, but Wiley just isn't there yet.
WILEY'S DAD. Coach...
COACH DAVIS. My name's Earl, Mr. Carson.
WILEY'S DAD. Okay, Earl...
COACH DAVIS. I've seen the kid's scores, he's on the right track, but he needs another year at least.
WILEY'S DAD. I haven't seen any scores. Are they bad?
COACH DAVIS. Look, there's nothing to get uptight about. Come on, let's go over his record. Sit down. (*He hands Wiley's dad the scores.*) See, Wiley is doing real good, he's just about ready to move up. Just give him some time, that's all.
WILEY'S DAD. Yeah, I see what you mean. I think. I don't know much about sports. Is this basketball?
COACH DAVIS. Football. You look like you could us a drink, man. (*Reaches offstage and magically produces a liquor drink, which he hands to Wiley's dad.*)
WILEY'S DAD. Probably could. (*Downs the entire drink.*) I guess I let it get to me. You know how it is, raising those boys by myself.
COACH DAVIS. You divorced?
WILEY'S DAD. Yeah.
COACH DAVIS. That's tough.
WILEY'S DAD. You're telling me...
COACH DAVIS. Another?
WILEY'S DAD. Sure...

(*COACH DAVIS reaches offstage and produces another drink, this time a big colorful girly drink, preferably with an umbrella and a straw, which he hands to Wiley's dad, who downs it.*)

COACH DAVIS. Lot a things you got to teach a young guy. They gettin' horny yet?
WILEY'S DAD. What do you mean?
COACH DAVIS. You know what I mean. Kids at that age. Remember how it was, getting real stiff, wondering what to do about it...
WILEY'S DAD. I see what you're talking about.
COACH DAVIS. Do you?

WILEY'S DAD. Sure. Those were the days weren't they? Man I used to come five, six times a day. How about you?

COACH DAVIS. Still do sometimes...

WILEY'S DAD. Spend all my time thinking about co...er... pussy...

COACH DAVIS. Wondering about how to get rid of all that cream...

WILEY'S DAD. Yeah...

COACH DAVIS. Looks like you're throwing a hard on, John.

WILEY'S DAD. Looks like, Coach...Earl...

COACH DAVIS. That's okay, you can call me Coach. I'll be your coach. (*Takes off his shorts, revealing a jock strap.*) Nobody's around. Nobody, Mr. Carson. Come on. Cut loose....

(*MUSIC: Porn Music. COACH DAVIS pulls WILEY'S DAD up by the tie. They furiously pull off each others' clothes until they're down to jockstraps. WILEY'S DAD's shoes are still on, pants around his ankles. COACH DAVIS puts WILEY'S DAD on his desk facing the audience, then moves behind him.*)

COACH DAVIS. Before you work out, you have to warm up and stretch.

(*COACH DAVIS reaches around and puts his fingers in WILEY'S DAD's mouth and stretches it, almost like a dentist. WILEY'S DAD tries to talk during this.*)

WILEY'S DAD. (*Unintelligible.*) It's important to stretch before physical activity.

COACH DAVIS. Now drop and give me twenty...eight inches at a time.

(*COACH DAVIS shoves WILEY'S DAD down so his head is hanging over the back of the desk, away from the audience, then positions himself to receive a blowjob. [This is all masked from the audience by the desk.] He talks to WILEY'S DAD throughout. WILEY'S DAD pops his head up for each of his lines.*)

COACH DAVIS. How do you like that dick?

WILEY'S DAD. I'm enjoying your dick!

COACH DAVIS. Nice, juicy, hot fucking dick.

WILEY'S DAD. It is nice!

COACH DAVIS. You've done it before. You like sucking that thick dick.

WILEY'S DAD. I won't lie - I'm enjoying sucking your nice, juicy, hot, thick fucking dick!

COACH DAVIS. On your back! I'm going to stretch your hamstrings.

(*COACH DAVIS pushes WILEY'S DAD into a sitting position, then spins him around so his face is hanging over the desk, facing the audience, and his ass is pointing upstage. He brings WILEY'S DAD's legs, still with pants and dress shoes on, up onto his shoulders and mounts him.)*

COACH DAVIS. Time to put one between the goal posts.

(COACH DAVIS enters WILEY'S DAD and fucks him vigorously. SOUND: Crowds cheering them on.)

WILEY'S DAD. Yes! Shoot that free throw thru the goal posts! Dribble the puck! Knock it out of the park! Knock the puck into home base! Fastball into the endzone! Score! Score! Score!

(They orgasm. LIGHTS SHIFT.)

Scene Ten

(ON THE ROAD - WILEY'S VAN.)

WILEY. And the next day I was on the varsity team. *(Realizes where he is.)* Hey, look Sam! Water! We made it from Yuma to the ocean in one afternoon!

(OCEAN. WILEY pulls over and gets out of the van. He pulls SAM along behind him on a leash.)

WILEY. Southern California. Man, this is beautiful. Go run, Sam. Enjoy the California beach. *(He unleashes Sam, then tosses him offstage.)* If only I could share it with...

(FLASHBACK LIGHTS. SOUND: War sounds. VIETNAM. WILEY moves over to JACK, a soldier who lies dying on the ground.)

JACK. *(Weakly:)* Wiley...
WILEY. Take it easy, Jack. It's gonna be okay!
JACK. Wiley...
WILEY. Take it easy, Jack! It will be okay! Hold on...
JACK. Wiley, it didn't work out. Promise me you won't forget me...
WILEY. Jack!
JACK. Just...just let somebody else in someday.
WILEY. Jack, you're gonna pull through...
JACK. Promise me! *(Dies.)*

(SOUND out. WILEY, broken hearted, slowly gets up, salutes JACK's body, then walks away. SOUND back in.)

JACK. *(Revived.)* Promise me you won't be alone! Let someone else in....

(WILEY races back to JACK.)

WILEY. It's a promise! It's a promise man!
JACK. Promise... Bright lights! Guns! Vietnam! *(He dies.)*
WILEY. *(Waits for a moment. Nudges Jack's body with his foot. When he's sure Jack is dead:)* Nooooooo!

Scene Eleven

(ON THE ROAD - HANK'S TRUCK. HANK drives down the road listening to the radio. LIGHTS UP RADIO STATION. FEMALE EVANGELIST is talking to her flock.)

FEMALE EVANGELIST. I'll tell ya something. We got another new show coming up on TV. It's a good one. It's called "Bowling for Sinners." It's a good one! We line up sinners in a bowling alley, instead of pins, and we take big rocks instead of balls and see how many we can kill! *(Sings.)* One day at a time, sweet Jesus..."

(HANK changes the radio station. FEMALE EVANGELIST becomes an EMERGENCY BROADCASTER reads a safety bulletin.)

EMERGENCY BROADCASTER. Here's a bulletin from the California Highway Patrol, or "CHiPs" as I'm told they're known. Ninety mile an hour winds along the coast. All roads have been closed between San Diego and Los Angeles. Drivers are advised to pull over to the side of the road until the early hours of the morning. This is an emergency bulletin from the California Highway Patrol. Take care, people.

(HANK pulls over.)

HANK. Well, if every single road between San Diego and Los Angeles is closed, I'd better sleep here on the side of the freeway.

(HANK turns off the truck. LIGHTS GROW DIM so we can barely see anything. After a few moments, a group of GAGE MEN, one with a flashlight, enters. Now the only light source is the flashlight. The GAGE MEN knock on HANK's window. HANK wakes up and immediately points a gun and a flashlight at the men.)

HANK. You better have a good reason for knockin' on my window, or my pals Smith and Wesson are gonna do the talkin' for me.

(HANK shines the flashlight on each of the men's crotches, one after another as they unbutton their pants.)

HANK. Damn! Three big dicks in the middle of a wind storm. I said a "wind storm…"

(*SOUND: Wind storm.*)

HANK. I love the Pacific Coast Highway! Won't need this gun to have sex with three strangers in the middle of nowhere.

(*HANK and the GAGE MEN go at it. The sex scene plays out with the flashlight shining on the men's faces, showing their reactions to what is going on [rather than showing the actual sex], and finally highlighting each of them as they orgasm.*)

Scene Twelve

(*L.A. TOOL AND DIE OFFICES. WILEY, dragging SAM on a leash, walks up to the L.A. Tool and Die offices. GAGE MEN cross wearing welding masks, carrying random tools, etc. The SOUNDS of machinery in the background. TANK approaches him.*)

TANK. Can I help you?
WILEY. I'm looking for the employment office.

(*GABE walks by with a slip of paper.*)

GABE. Got it! I start tomorrow! Now my dad can get off my back! (*Gives a Gage Man five, then exits.*)
TANK. You're in luck, they're hiring.
WILEY. I know. I left everything behind to work here.
TANK. It's on the other side of the lot over there. See where that guy came out?
WILEY. Yeah, thanks.

(*SFX :Car crash.*)

TANK. What the Hell?
GAGE MAN. That kid just flipped his car backing out of his parking space!

(*GABE staggers in, holding a steering wheel. He collapses on the ground. TANK and WILEY rush over.*)

WILEY. You okay, kid?
TANK. Doesn't look like nothin's broken.
GABE. Except the car!

TANK. (*Holds Gabe.*) Relax, it's okay.
GABE. It's my dad's car. He's gonna kill me!
TANK. I saw what happened. It wasn't your fault.
GABE. He's gonna go apeshit.
TANK. What's your name?
GABE. Gabe.
TANK. Gabe, I'm Tank. Do you want me to go with you to tell your dad?
GABE. I can't face him yet. Besides he's gone til tomorrow.
TANK. Where ya gonna go?
GABE. I don't know...
TANK. Come on, get up.
GABE. Huh?
TANK. You're gonna go with me. I'll get ya a beer and we'll get your shit together then we'll see.
GABE. At least they gave me the job.
TANK. See, ya got something.

(*TANK and GABE exit. HANK enters.*)

HANK. That sure was something how that kid flipped that car backing out of his parking space.
WILEY. What...what are you doing here?
HANK. Oh, you know, looking for a job. (*He's looking at Wiley's crotch.*)
WILEY. (*Pulling Hank's chin up.*) My eyes are up here.
HANK. (*Smitten.*) Right there on your face. (*Recovers.*) Anyway, I hear they're hiring. Got tired of the midwest, so thought I'd give L.A. a try.
SAM. Arf!
WILEY. Quiet! He is not!

(*JACK enters, unseen by HANK. FLASHBACK LIGHTS. SFX: War sounds.*)

JACK. Promise me, Wiley...
WILEY. I can't!
JACK. Promise me...just...just let somebody else in someday....
WILEY. I can't, Jack!
SAM. Arf! Arf! Arf!
WILEY. I said be quiet!
HANK. Who you talkin' to, Wiley?
WILEY. (*Hissy fit:*) Not my dog, and not my flashback dead lover! I'm not talking to anybody! And I'm not talking to you! (*Races out.*)
SAM. (*As he's dragged out:*) Arf! Arf! Arf! Arf!

(*SOUND out. JACK exits. LIGHTS RESTORE.*)

HANK. Wiley, wait! Damn it! I come all the way to L.A. just to keep chasin' that man. I'd give up, but I coulda sworn that dog was trying to tell me something.

GAGE MAN. Hiring office closes in five minutes!

HANK. Wiley'll have to wait. I got a job to get! (*Exits.*)

Scene Thirteen

(*TANK'S HOUSE. GABE enters in a towel, post shower. TANK follows.*)

GABE. This is a great double wide, Tank. Oh, man, this shag carpet feels amazing! (*Sees stereo set up.*) Wow, that's a great reel-to-reel! How much did that cost?

TANK. I bought that for fifty whole dollars.

GABE. (*Notices art.*) Hey, I didn't know you did string art! (*Turns around to see Tank without his towel.*)

TANK. Get out of that wet towel.

(*GABE whips off his towel in one motion. SOUND: Whip crack.*)

TANK. Good thing I got two bathrobes. (*Tosses Gabe a bathrobe, then puts one on himself, leaving it untied and open.*) Nothing like a hot shower to take the edge of, huh?

GABE. Uh, yeah. You always take showers with your guests?

TANK. Of course! There's a water shortage in California, ain't you heard? Can't be wasting water on separate showers.

GABE. Wow, you're smart.

TANK. Besides, how would ya get your back clean if ya didn't have a bud to scrub it for ya?

GABE. And why did we wash each others' chests?

TANK. That's called teamwork. You gotta work together to get the job done. Normally we all shower at work after the shift, but since we hightailed it outta there after the wreck, I didn't get my shower. I'm the shift manager, and now you're on my crew, so figured I'd start showing you the ropes.

GABE. You been real nice to me, Tank. I can't thank you enough.

TANK. We'll see about that. How about a beer? That hot shower took some of the edge of, but I can tell you're still feeling...a little nervous. (*Gets two beers.*) You old enough to drink?

GABE. Oh, sure. I'm starting college in the fall. I just haven't ever had alcohol before.

TANK. Drink up.

(*GABE chugs his entire beer. As he does...*)

TANK. You're gonna be right at home in college.

GABE. (*Finished with the beer.*) Wow, that went down easy.

TANK. (*To audience:*) Do I really have to say it?

GABE. You sure you don't mind my staying over?

TANK. Hell, no. I didn't have no plans. Now get on your feet.

GABE. What?

TANK. Help me make this rolling set piece into the bed. (*NOTE: In the original production a rolling set piece was used for various pieces of furniture. "Set piece" can be changed to "couch" if needed.*)

GABE. Oh.

TANK. You don't want to bunk with me, do ya?

GABE. I don't want to be no trouble.

TANK. I'd let you sleep in with me, but I thrash around a lot, have a hard on most of the night. In fact, I think I'm getting one now. (*His hard dick instantly makes a tent in the bathrobe. He bangs it on the bed or the set for emphasis - knock, knock, knock! [NOTE: This effect is created with a rod sewn into the robe that the actor can control.]*) You don't have to say anything. Your dick is saying it for you.

(*GABE's hard dick instantly makes a tent in his bathrobe [using the same effect]. NOTE: This next sex scene is staged with the audience seeing nothing except the actors touching the hard dicks thru the robes, or with the actors masking the action by holding their robes open at just the right angle, leaving what's happening inside the robes to the imagination of the audience.*)

GABE. (*A beat.*) Swordfight! (*He excitedly whacks his cock against Tank's several times.*)

TANK. (*Wincing.*) Okay, why don't we polish these swords first? (*He strokes Gabe's hard cock.*)

GABE. Oh, oh! Oh, that feels much better than a sword fight. Yes! Oh, yeah, oh...(*starts to sing.*) "Some say love..."

TANK. You don't have a lot of experience, do you?

GABE. No.

TANK. Well, let me give you a lesson or two. (*Reaches into Gabe's robe and starts manipulating his dick.*) How's that? Uh, huh? And that? And then you do this, and this feels good...

GABE. (*Simultaneous.*) Oh, yeah! Oh, wow, that's...oh, my God, that's amazing...

TANK. Okay, remember, team work. It's time to take care of your shift manager.

(*TANK opens his robe. GABE reaches in and violently yanks on TANK's cock.*)

TANK. Aaaauugh! Ouch! No! Slow! Slow down! Slow down! Okay, first take that...Okay, yeah, that's good...Now the other way...Yeah, nice, man that feels good...Now grab those...Gently! Yeah, both at the same time....Oh, fuck, yeah...

(*SOUND: Jackhammers.*)

GABE. (*Simultaneous.*) Oh, okay...Like this? Okay, and like this? And these? Pull these and do this...
TANK. Okay, same time...

(*They reach into each other's robes and jack each other off to climax. SOUND: End of shift factory whistle.*)

Scene Fourteen

(*L.A. TOOL AND DIE. HANK, WILEY and the GAGE MEN enter read to work.*)

HANK. You over your little...spell?
WILEY. I'm just fine. I...I just...

(*TANK pokes his head in.*)

TANK. (*Off.*) Alright men, time to get to work.

(*The men start to work, using random tools. We don't really know what they're doing, and neither do they - it's just sort of generic hammering, screwing, sawing, but they do it for about ten seconds, then --.*)

TANK. (*Off.*) Lunch time!

(*The GAGE MEN cheer and immediately start taking off their clothes as they exit. HANK and WILEY are left behind.*)

HANK. Well, here we are. Alone at last. And you have to talk to me. Your dog said so.
WILEY. (*Under his breath:*) Stupid Sam...
HANK. So, let's talk. You start.
WILEY. Well --
HANK. Did anything interesting happen on your trip?
WILEY. I had --
HANK. See any sights? How's your dog? Man, aren't much for talkin', are ya?
WILEY. Uh. Well, remember what I said about sport fucking when we first met? Well, I've been trying it out a little since then.

HANK. And?

WILEY. I think I might have gotten a gas station attendant fired.

HANK. Nah, ya only blinded him in one eye.

WILEY. Oh, good. That's a relief.

HANK. Wish my eye'd been on the receiving end of your dick.

WILEY. Hank, you're real good at sweet talk. I just have some things I have to figure out.

HANK. Wiley, you know what I want. But I don't want to force it on ya.

WILEY. You've been real good about not leaning on me these three times we've been around each other.

HANK. If it's gonna happen, it will.

WILEY. I guess...

HANK. Hey, did I ever tell you about my millions?

WILEY. What do you mean?

HANK. Sure, I got 'em. I've been putting away everything I ever earned on some land out in Porterville. Sending it in to the land office for years. Oh, I know, seems mighty convenient since I've never talked about it and it just happens to be in the same place a total stranger I've been following ended up. Still never seen it. Gonna go up this weekend and take a look at it. Finally paid it off the other day. (*Kneels, feels the ground as if he's on his land.*) Gonna retire, man, raise me some oranges, live the good life. I'm getting too old for this donkey work, this independent contractor shit. You wanna come up? Take a look at it with me?

WILEY. I don't know...

HANK. (*Grabs Wiley's hand.*) Hey man, I'm not asking you to marry me. You know how many times a day you say "No"? No, no, no, no. Tomorrow's Saturday, right? I'm gonna be at the land office at noon to pick up that deed. You wanna come? If not, well... It's time to get back to work. Ain't these glasses a bitch? (*Puts on his safety glasses and walks off.*)

WILEY. (*Whispers:*) Damn you...

(*JACK enters. FLASHBACK LIGHTS. SOUND: War sounds.*)

JACK. You promised, Wiley...

WILEY. I know. I just...

(*TANK pokes his head in. JACK exits. LIGHTS RESTORE. SOUND out.*)

TANK. Okay men, back to work!

(*The GAGE MEN enter and resume their fake working.*)

TANK. Come on, Wiley. Get your shirt off. There's work to be done!

WILEY. (*Takes off his shirt.*) So, what exactly do we do here?

(*All the GAGE MEN look at WILEY as if he's asked the forbidden question.*)

TANK. We... make things and do stuff. Get back to work!

Scene Fifteen

(*LAND OFFICE. HANK enters and approaches the FEMALE CLERK.*)

FEMALE CLERK. Can I help you?
HANK. I'm here to pick up the deed on the Woodman property up Porterville way.
FEMALE CLERK. (*Immediately hands him the deed and a map.*) Here you go. Hope you didn't pay much for it.
HANK. Why do you say that?
FEMALE CLERK. (*Shouts to her coworkers offstage:*) Hey kids, whaddya got to say about the Woodman property up near Porterville.
COWORKERS (*Off. Raucous laughter.*) AH HA HA HA HA!!
FEMALE CLERK. You have yourself a nice day, jackass. (*Exits.*)
HANK. Jovial bunch. (*Looks at watch.*) Twelve straight up. No Wiley. I'll give him ten more minutes.

(*HANK leans against the wall. A door with a "Men's Room" sign appears. MUSIC: Porn music. A GAGE MAN enters, looks around furtively, adjusts his crotch, then enters the men's room. A second GAGE MAN appears, looks around, adjusts, enters the men's room. And then a third. And a fourth. And a fifth, this time the first GAGE MAN, but wearing a slightly different piece of costume - hat? Glasses? Mustache? And then a sixth, seventh and eight, all wearing new, distinct costume pieces - janitor, cowboy, business man, mailman, etc. The feel should be a long line of men entering, but obviously the same four actors just changing something simple. Nine, ten, eleven.*)

HANK. That's one popular bathroom.

(*HANK exits into the men's room. WILEY enters.*)

WILEY. I'm here! Hank? Fuck! Missed him!

(*The sounds of sex can be heard from the men's room.*)

WILEY. What the...?

(*WILEY enters the men's room. The sounds of sex get much louder. The sex sounds build, build, build until everybody orgasms simultaneously. [NOTE: Actors should improvise the sounds of the orgy taking place off-stage, adding laugh lines, directions, etc..]*)

ALL. (*Off.*) I'm cumming!!! Aaaauuugh! (*Unison.*) OH, YEAH!!!!

(*One after another, again double, tripling with costume changes, the GAGE MEN all enter the stage from the men's room, zip up their pants, then exit. After the final GAGE MAN leaves the men's room, the FEMALE CLERK exits the men's room.*)

FEMALE CLERK. That's the women's room, you bastards! (*She fixes the "Men's Room" sign to reveal it is actually the "Women's Room". She stomps off.*)

(*HANK and WILEY enter the stage from the men's room. HANK has his arm around WILEY's shoulders in a friendly gesture.*)

WILEY. That was real special, Hank. But one romantic date doesn't mean I'm ready to give myself over to you.
HANK. I'm just glad you made it. But if I was bein' honest, when I watched all those men excavating your throat like there was gold in your guts and their cocks were the shovels, I heard wedding bells.
WILEY. Don't get to sweet talkin' me. I just came by because I thought there'd be more room in my van than in your truck.
HANK. Is that so?
WILEY. It is. You want a ride or not?
HANK. I want a ride. 'Specially if you're drivin'.
WILEY. Then let's go.

(*HANK and WILEY cross to WILEY's van.*)

Scene Sixteen

(*WILEY'S VAN. SAM pops up in then van.*)

SAM. Arf!
WILEY. Scoot over, Sam. We got company.
SAM. Arf! Arf! Arf!
WILEY. Don't mind him. His one mission in life is to embarrass me.
HANK. What? He just said that he doesn't mind moving over for a handsome, available stud like me.
WILEY. (*Stunned:*) Lucky guess.
HANK. Was it?

WILEY. We better get a move on before it gets dark. (*Indicates a big "X" on Hank's map.*) It's a long trip.

(*WILEY starts the van. They drive for ten seconds. The LIGHTS instantly drop to nighttime. A GAGE MAN enters and drops a big "X" on the stage floor. The van stops. We're now at HANK'S LAND. They get out of the van.*)

WILEY. We're here.
HANK. Awfully dry for oranges out here, don't ya think?
WILEY. You sure this is it?
HANK. (*Referring to the "X"s on the map and ground.*) That's what it says. Oranges? This land couldn't grow lint. I don't have sense to pour piss out of a boot! I'll kill 'em!
WILEY. Hank...
HANK. Just go!
WILEY. Hank...
HANK. You don't understand, I quit my fucking job!
WILEY. Hank, you're gonna be alright...
HANK. Stop trying to make me feel better! You ain't my man, you've made that perfectly clear. I don't need your pity, I don't need your talking dog, and I don't need you! (*Runs off crying like a girl.*)
WILEY. Hank, wait! (*A beat.*) What if I need you? (*Exits.*)

Scene Seventeen

(*HARRY'S OFFICE. VIC enters to find HARRY at his desk.*)

HARRY. Vic! Where ya been?! I haven't seen you for weeks!
VIC. I was at that men's bar ya sent me to. Been there every night for two weeks, and you're right - nothing!
HARRY. Nothing?
VIC. Nothing! Well, there was one thing...

(*GAGE MAN enters with tub of Crisco.*)

GAGE MAN. It's butter flavored!
HARRY. (*Unbuttoning his pants.*) Kid, I hope ya got small hands....

Scene Eighteen

(*WILEY'S VAN. FLASHBACK LIGHTS and MUSIC. HANK and WILEY enter. They lip sync to these new lines.*)

HANK V.O. Are you sure we need another flashback.

(*The DIRECTOR'S VOICE comes in from nowhere. HANK and WILEY react with surprise.*)

DIRECTOR V.O. Yes! We have a quick costume change, so we need to stall for time.
SAM V.O. Arf! Arf!
WILEY V.O. Oh, okay.
HANK V.O. (*Sticks his fingers in Wiley's mouth.*) You sure about that?
WILEY V.O. I gotta go to LA.
HANK V.O. See ya.
WILEY V.O. Bye.

(*HANK and WILEY exit.*)

Scene Nineteen

(*L.A. TOOL & DIE. GABE enters to find TANK working.*)

GABE. Hey, Tank! I don't know what you said to my dad, but he wasn't mad at all! In fact, he bought me my own car!
TANK. You dad can seem cold-hearted, but he warms up in a hot shower.
GABE. I guess my dad and I are more alike than I thought.
TANK. Now get back to work!

(*TANK and GABE exit.*)

Scene Twenty

(*HANK'S LAND. WILEY, carrying a bottle of Jack Daniels, helps HANK back to the van. They are both drunk.*)

WILEY. Okay, you had your cry. Let's take a look at that deed and see if there's anything we can do.
HANK. Where'd you get this bottle of Jack? We're in the middle of the desert.
WILEY. I'm very resourceful. Now give me that deed. (*Reads deed.*) Looks like they really got ya. The way this is written, there's not much you can do about it. You got water rights.
HANK. Shit, in this desert? I bet the nearest water main is fifty miles away.
WILEY. You got airspace rights. You got commercial rights.
HANK. I'm supposed to be up to my ass in oranges.
WILEY. You can get your job back, Hank.
HANK. You think?
WILEY. Are you kidding? You're the best guy on the job. You're reliable. You know what you're doing. And you're easy...easy to...

HANK. Hey Wiley, you sure got a glow on.

WILEY. No, I'm serious...You're easy...to like...

HANK. Is that what it is, kid? The old man's easy to like? You fucker. I love you.

(*JACK appears, holding SAM. FLASHBACK LIGHTS. SOUND: War sounds. They silently motion for WILEY to take the leap. WILEY moves over to JACK and holds him.*)

JACK. Go on, Wiley. For me.

SAM. Arf!

WILEY. If you can't listen to your dog and your dead lover's ghost, who can you listen to?

JACK. I'm so happy for you, Wiley. You finally let someone in. (*A beat. Tenderly:*) Do you mind if I watch and jack off?

WILEY. It wouldn't be the same if you weren't.

HANK. You talking to your dead lover again?

WILEY. Not any more. I love you, too, Hank.

(*JACK and SAM move upstage to watch. HANK and WILEY embrace. MUSIC: Romantic music. A GAGE MAN brings out a blanket and pillows. HANK and WILEY drunkenly disrobe each other and slip under the blanket. HANK and WILEY begin to make love. JACK watches and masturbates. A GAGE MAN enters.*)

GAGE MAN. Gentlemen and gentlemen, Charlene.

(*CHARLENE and two BACK UP DANCERS enter. She sings "I've Never Been to Me" as the men make love. JACK orgasms, sending way too much cum flying across the stage as LIGHTS FADE.*)

Scene Twenty-One

(*HANK'S LAND. WILEY wakes up to find HANK gone.*)

WILEY. Hank? Where are ya? He's gone. That son of a bitch!

(*HANK enters with a mallet and a sign that reads "For Sale".*)

HANK. Mornin', Wiley. (*Crosses and exits.*)

WILEY. (*Dresses as he calls off to Hank.*) "For Sale"? How can you sell this land? You've only had it for a day!

(*We hear the sign being pounded into the ground as HANK yells back to WILEY.*)

HANK. (*Off.*) This piece of dirt ain't worth shit. Maybe I can convince some other sucker to take it on and get my money back.
WILEY. Hank, you can't sell this land. (*A beat.*) No, seriously, you can't sell it. It's worthless.
HANK. (*Off.*) Then I'll throw in a set of ginsu knives.
WILEY. That'll make it worth $19.99. Well, plus shipping and handling...

(*We hear pound, pound, pound, then a geyser of water erupting from the ground.*)

HANK. (*Off.*) Thar she blows! Whoo hoo!
WILEY. What the Hell?!

(*HANK enters.*)

HANK. I hit water! (*A bucketful of water splashes him.*)
WILEY. Water?! (*A bucketful of water splashes him from the other direction.*)
HANK. This ain't no desert! It's an orange grove to be!
WILEY. You got your millions, Hank!

(*HANK grabs WILEY in a manly hug.*)

HANK. I had my fortune already, er...uh...
WILEY. Wiley!
HANK. Wiley.

(*They kiss as an orange tree appears in the distance and the LIGHTS GO TO BLACK.*)

END OF PLAY

CAMP KILLSPREE

A gay slasher comedy play by

Sean Abley

The mayhem that is Camp Killspree. (L to R, front) Angelo Petronio, Mitchel Fain, E. Millard Jones, John Cardone. (Back) Brad Boehmke, Fred Gloor, Joey Meyer, Todd Ball and Elliot Jordan.

Camp Killspree, Bailiwick Repertory, Chicago IL 1994 (newspaper scans)

148

ACKNOWLEDGEMENTS

Camp Killspree was first performed at Bailiwick Repertory (David Zak, Executive Director), Chicago, IL, on July 5, 1994 as part of the Pride Performance Series. The production was directed by Sean Abley. Repertory Stage Manager – Mitchell Sellers. Production Stage Manager – Patricia Sutherland. Fight Choreographer – Kirk Pynchon. The cast was as follows:

CLIFFORD......................	Joey Meyer
NORMAN.........................	Fred Gloor
RICHARD........................	Brad Boehmke
STEVE...........................	Elliott Jordan
TIM.............................	Todd Ball
TERRY...........................	John Cardone
JACK............................	E. Millard Jones
CHUCK..........................	Mitchell J. Fain
CARLOS.........................	Angelo Petronio
GARY...........................	Shawn Courtney
ANDREW........................	Rick Beech
HITCHHIKER....................	Fred Gloor
ROSE...........................	Joey Meyer
COPS...........................	Fred Gloor, Brad Boehmke

SPECIAL THANKS: The Factory Theatre, John Rent at the Flower Cart, Roscoe's Café, Mike Meredith, Nick Digilio from ALIVE, Michelle J. Rappaport DDS, Maureen Marrinac MD, and Party Productions.

CHARACTERS

CLIFFORD – 70's gay porn star type
NORMAN – Ditto, until he comes back as the Hitchhiker.
RICHARD – Ditto, until he comes back at the end of the play

STEVE – A clone, any age but probably in his 20's.
TIM – Ditto. You can't really tell him apart from Steve.

TERRY – Denist, well-heeled and maybe a little stuffy, but not obnoxiously so. A grown up, probably in his 30's or 40's.
JACK – Terry's boyfriend, a little bit more of a free spirit, constantly trying to get Terry to loosen up. 30's or 40's.

CHUCK – The single guy, the "Final Girl" of this movie. Good looking, but a big of a complainer, and a little bit psychic.

CARLOS – a Latin actor type. 20's or 30's.
GARY – Carlos's boyfriend, a fratboy type. 20's or 30's.

ANDREW – a gay nerd until he takes his clothes off, then he's an incredibly hot gay nerd.

HITCHHIKER – Originally thought to be Norman from the prologue, but could be just a random crazy guy.

ROSE – A career waitress. Played by a man in the original production, but not a requirement.

THE KILLER – Should be played by several different actors that are obviously different sizes throughout the show.

COP ONE
COP TWO

TIME

Twenty years ago in 1970, and twenty years later in 1984. Yes, the math doesn't add up.

SETTING

Hard Log Men's Resort, and Camp Community.

CAMP KILLSPREE

By Sean Abley

Scene One

(*SLIDE - "1970 - Twenty Years Ago." LIGHTS UP. HARD LOG MEN'S RESORT. Twenty years ago. Bearskin rug, fireplace, clothing optional, all the requisite elements for a "Men Only" resort. Outside, it's pouring rain. We hear SFX: car pulling up and some 70s dance music from the car radio. The car and radio cut out at the same time, car doors open and shut, then CLIFFORD and NORMAN making their way to the house in the rain.*)

CLIFFORD. (*Off.*) Hurry up! Watch out for that puddle, it's really deep!

(*SFX: splash.*)

NORMAN (*Off.*) Wow, that puddle's really deep!

(*CLIFFORD and NORMAN enter, soaking wet.*)

CLIFFORD. Hurry up! I'm soaked.
NORMAN. You're soaked? That puddle must have been waist deep.
CLIFFORD. Take off your shoes. I don't want wet footprints all over the floor.

(*NORMAN stays at the door, takes off his shoes while CLIFFORD takes off all his clothes.*)

NORMAN. This place is beautiful. What's it called?
CLIFFORD. Hard Log Men's Resort.
NORMAN. You and Richard own this whole place?
CLIFFORD. The whole thing. Right down the middle. So if one of us dies the other one will get everything. (*Does a take as SFX: Crack of thunder*) Let's not talk about Richard.
NORMAN. Dick.
CLIFFORD. He prefers Richard.
NORMAN. Well, I prefer dick.
CLIFFORD. Ah, the witty sexual innuendo wordplay that makes up the homosexual lexicon.
NORMAN. Um, what?
CLIFFORD. Never mind.
NORMAN. I want to own property some day. My dream is to have my own gay sports bar. I'm going to call it "Balls." Because there are a lot of balls in sports.
CLIFFORD. You don't say.

NORMAN. No, I just did.

CLIFFORD. You just did what?

NORMAN. Say. You said, "You don't say." But I did say.

CLIFFORD. Norman, your cunning linguistics are wasted on me.

NORMAN. My cunninglinwhatstics?

CLIFFORD. And you as well, apparently. Are you just going to stand there?

NORMAN. Well, my shoes are off, but my clothes are going to drip all over the floor if I'm off the mat.

(*CLIFFORD lies on the rug across the room.*)

CLIFFORD. Hmmm, that's a problem. I'm not sure how you're going to get all the way over here to the rug without getting the floor wet.

NORMAN. Oh, wait, I have an idea. (*Strips off his clothes.*)

CLIFFORD. Good answer, Norman. You are a very wise man.

NORMAN. Now what?

CLIFFORD. I take that back. Come over here.

(*NORMAN moves over to CLIFFORD on the rug. They start making out, but NORMAN keeps nervously looking toward the door.*)

CLIFFORD. What's wrong?

NORMAN. What if Richard catches us? He has a really bad temper. I remember back when we were dating he kicked in our TV screen when they switched 'Darrins" on "Betwitched."

CLIFFORD. Stop being paranoid. I'm just fucking his ex while he's away for the weekend. What could go wrong?

NORMAN. He'll kill us if he comes home early.

CLIFFORD. He won't get home early.

(*RICHARD enters.*)

RICHARD. I'm home early!

CLIFFORD. Shit.

NORMAN. Hi, Richard! It's me!

RICHARD. Clifford?

NORMAN. No, Norman!

CLIFFORD. Um…Thank God you're home! I was attacked and knocked unconscious, and Norman just happened to be in the neighborhood of our secluded men's only resort and saved me.

NORMAN. He's joking. He sucked my dick in the diner's bathroom in town and said we should finish off here. Hi!

CLIFFORD. Can't you *ever* play along?

RICHARD. What the hell is going on here?!

CLIFFORD. Richard, wait, this isn't what you think.

RICHARD. This isn't you fucking my ex because you thought I was going to be gone all weekend?

CLIFFORD. Okay, sure. But there are extenuating circumstances! His dick is really nice!

RICHARD. We agreed—no playing around one-on-one with random tricks. Threeways or fourgies with both of us only!

CLIFFORD. Richard—

RICHARD. You've made me look like an idiot for the last time! You're gonna pay for this!

CLIFFORD. Richard, cut it out! You're scaring me!

RICHARD. Oh, I'll cut it out, alright!

(RICHARD grabs a small chainsaw just outside the door and starts it.)

NORMAN. Shit!

CLIFFORD. Richard, wait—!

NORMAN. Now I'll never own "Balls!"

(BLACKOUT. In the dark we hear their screams and the chainsaw. OPENING CREDITS. Typical horror film music as the credits roll. The credits should be real, listing the writer, director, producer, cast and crew of this production, but which roles the actors play should be left out. The last slide/credit should read: "1984 - Twenty Years Later." CREDITS AND MUSIC FADE OUT.)

Scene Two

(STEVE AND TIM'S APARTMENT. STEVE and TIM are packing. Today they wear white t-shirts that both say "Bottom," cutoffs, and boots.)

STEVE. How long are we going to be there?

TIM. Two months.

STEVE. Okay, so we've got ten white t-shirts, ten white tank tops, ten black t-shirts, two pairs cut-offs, and sixteen pairs white crew socks...

TIM. ...diamond studs, small hoop earrings, freedom rings, cock rings...

STEVE. ...hand towels, condoms in bulk...

STEVE / TIM. Thank God for Costco!

TIM. *(Commercial:)* Wet personal lubricant, two liter family size...

STEVE. And one jockstrap each. Phew! All this packing makes me thirsty.

TIM. Here, drink this. *(Hands a can of Coke to STEVE with the logo conspicuously displayed.)*

STEVE. *(Drinks soda.)* Mmmmm this product placement is delicious. Is this an off-brand soda?

TIM. Nope! *(Commercial:)* It's the real thing.

STEVE. We better get going. It's supposed to rain and I want to get there before it gets dark.

TIM. What's the name of this place again?

Scene Three

(*TERRY AND JACK'S APARTMENT. JACK and TERRY are packing.*)

JACK. Camp Community. And it's a great cause. You know, gay teenagers.

TERRY. I know, but aren't we a little old for this? I mean, all that ever happened at camp was drinking, and smoking pot, and skinny dipping, and sex all the time...

JACK. And?

TERRY. And did you see the paper today? (*Holds up newspaper and reads the headline:*) "Homicidal Lunatic Escapes Asylum." (*SFX: Thunder crack. He flips paper over and continues to read:*) "Stay Away From Summer Camp." (*SFX: Thunder crack. He turns paper over, reads headline on the back:*) "Seriously, He Will Kill You." (*SFX: Thunder crack.*)

JACK. That's funny. There isn't a cloud in the sky. Anyway, as long as he's not a *homo*-cidal lunatic, we'll be fine. Come on, loosen up, doctor. Unbutton that top button.

TERRY. But it's still daylight out. Chest hair is for evenings and weekends.

JACK. This is going to be fun. Help me get this stuff into the car. We have to be at Carlos and Gary's in fifteen minutes.

Scene Four

(*CARLOS AND GARY'S APARTMENT. CARLOS and GARY are packing. Their friend CHUCK mopes around their house.*)

CHUCK. But I don't want to go.

CARLOS. Why not, Chuck?

CHUCK. Well, you know I'm a little bit psychic, and (*Spooky, reverb, semi-psychic voice:*) I have a bad feeling about this trip. (*Normal voice.*) Besides, I'm totally going to be the— (*Counts on his fingers.*)—seventh wheel.

GARY. You are not.

CHUCK. I are, too. Everybody else is going to have their boyfriend or lover there, and I'm stuck with Mrs. Thumb and her four daughters.

GARY. Why do you name your jack off hand a woman?

CHUCK. What do you call jacking off?

GARY. An encore presentation of *Hand*-el's "Messiah."

CHUCK. Well, how cultured of you. I'm sure your high school music teacher is thrilled every time you masturbate.

GARY. Thanks. Now I'll be thinking of Mrs. Granger every morning in the shower.

CHUCK / CARLOS. Eeeeiiww.

CHUCK. Carlos, please. Don't make me go.

CARLOS. Don't be such a pussy. Besides, Gary and I have arranged for you to have a, um, bunk mate for the summer.

CHUCK. What?! No way. *No way.* I am not going on a two-month blind date with some loser *mus grande* and the six of you playing matchmaker. Count me out. I'd rather die alone. (*A beat.*) Is he cute?

GARY. He is… loaded with personality.

CHUCK. Oh, God, he's ugly.

CARLOS. He's not ugly.

CHUCK. Then he's a closet case.

CARLOS. He's not in the closet.

CHUCK. Then he's a Republican.

CARLOS. I just told you he's not in the closet. (*SFX: Doorbell.*) I got it! (*He exits.*)

CHUCK. You know how much I hate being set up. I swear, Gary, if this turns out bad, I'll murder you. (*Does a take as SFX: Thunder crack.*)

(*CARLOS enters with STEVE, TIM, TERRY, and JACK. There are "hellos" all around.*)

STEVE / TIM. What's wrong, Chuck?

CHUCK. Carlos and Gary set me up with some weirdo for the summer.

TERRY. Is he cute?

GARY. He's very… vivacious.

STEVE / TIM / TERRY / JACK. He's ugly.

GARY. He's not ugly. He's differently handsome.

JACK. So you invited Eve Arden.

(*SFX: Doorbell*)

GARY. He's letting us use his minivan, so behave. (*GARY exits.*)

JACK. We're being have.

CHUCK. You know, I'm suddenly not feeling well. Man, my stomach is a mess. Maybe I should just stay home.

CARLOS. Maybe Terry should examine you. Start with this prostate.

TERRY. I'm a dentist.

CARLOS. Considering Chuck's track record, I'm sure it's a straight shot to his molars from there anyway.

CHUCK. Laugh it up, but I'm not going.

JACK. But what about all those poor gay teenagers you'll be letting down? Each of us has a set of skills crucial for this camp to run well. Without you, the whole thing could fall apart.

CARLOS. Think of the children.

STEVE. Wait, Chuck has skills?

STEVEN / TIM. Name one.

CHUCK. Well, I am a little bit psychic. I actually knew who shot J.R.

JACK. That's… valuable…ish. And we also need someone to direct the talent show, so...

CHUCK. The talent show! (*Magnanimously.*) Well, if I must put aside my personal discomfort for the good of the children, then so be it. I have a lot of plans for our little theatrical extravaganza, and the first order of business will be casting. Of course I nominate myself for the lead—

TERRY. There's a lead in a talent show?

(*GARY enters.*)

GARY. Hey, everybody! Meet Andrew.

(*ANDREW enters in full nerd mode.*)

ANDREW. Hello, everyone. Sorry I'm late. I had to get a refill on my inhaler prescription.

(*All turn and look at CHUCK. SFX: Thunder crack. BLACKOUT.*)

Scene Five

(*IN THE VAN ON THE ROAD. All of our campers are crowded in, with ANDREW at the wheel.*)

ANDREW. Cow! Auto Bingo! Man, I am smoking you guys! In your face!

TERRY. You were right. This is a lot of fun.

CARLOS. Chuck, why aren't you playing Auto Bingo with the rest of us?

CHUCK. I'm reading this book on "How to Harness Your Psychic Power."

GARY. Why?

CHUCK. In the last scene I established I'm a little bit psychic, and I don't know, I just think it will come in handy later…

JACK. It's roasting in here.

STEVE / TIM. Can't we turn on the air conditioning?

TERRY. Good idea.

(*He reaches for the control, but ANDREW stops him.*)

ANDREW. Sorry. I can't have air conditioning. I'm allergic to freon.

CARLOS. Then roll down the windows.

ANDREW. Ooh, no. The wind shear wreaks havoc on my gas mileage.

CARLOS. Oh. Okay.

ANDREW. You're not eating back there, are you?

GARY. (*He is eating*) No.

ANDREW. Okay, because I don't want to get food on the floor.

JACK. So we can't eat, we can't roll down the window, we can't turn on the air conditioner, and we can't listen to the radio because it's a strain on the van's battery.

CHUCK. It's like a less fun Bataan Death March.

JACK. I'm pretty bored here. Why don't you tell us what we can do.

ANDREW. We could sing "Row, Row, Row Your Boat" in a round.

ALL. (*General disagreement.*)

ANDREW. The License Plate Game?

ALL. (*General disagreement.*)

ANDREW. (*Pulls out a spiral notebook.*) I could read my "Star Trek" Kirk/Spock gay slash fiction stories out loud.

ALL. NO!

GARY. Actually...

CARLOS. Shush!

TERRY. Hey, wait a minute. We brought a boom box and batteries. Let's listen to that.

ALL. Cool, great, excellent, right on, etc.

TERRY. I have a cassingle of [NAME OF SONG] right here.

(*TERRY pulls out the box and puts in the cassingle of some sort of 70's dance music that mirrors the song we heard in the prologue. [The original production used "Boogie Fever" by The Sylvers] They sing along, under their breath at first, then more and more energetically until we have a full-fledged song and dance floorshow that magically expands outside the van.*

A HITCHHIKER suddenly appears at the side of the road. He looks quite dangerous and frightening. He jogs alongside the van.)

JACK. Look! A hitchhiker!

(*The music instantly stops as everyone snaps back to their places in the van.*)

STEVE / TIM. He looks dangerous and frightening!

JACK. Let's pick him up.

ANDREW. I don't know...

TERRY. We could be asking for trouble by inviting a transient into the van.

JACK. Oh, stop. What's the worst that could happen? It's not like he's going to murder us this early in the play.

ANDREW. Well, okay. It's the least we could do, considering he's kept up with us doing sixty and all. (*Pulls the van over and stops.*) Come on in, stranger.

HITCHHIKER. Thanks! How about a hand in?

CHUCK. Here…

(*CHUCK holds out his hand to help HITCHHIKER in. As soon as they grasp hands, CHUCK has a vision. We hear SFX: chainsaw and the opening scene in voice over.*)

NORMAN (V.O). Shit!

CLIFFORD (V.O.). Richard, wait—!

NORMAN (V.O.). Now I'll never own "Balls!"

(*The vision is over.*)

CHUCK. Oh my God!

GARY. What?

CHUCK. I just had a—

HITCHHIKER. Hey, the Sylvers! That brings back memories. That must have been almost twenty years ago!

JACK. Memories?

HITCHHIKER. Yeah, I musta been about twenty-eight when I first heard that song.

CHUCK. Wait, "Boogie Fever" came out in 1975… is a random thing that I know. The prologue was 1970, and it's 1984 now, so …

CARLOS. Wow. Please don't take this wrong, but you don't look that old.

HITCHHIKER. Well, thank you. I use a moisturizing soap. It keeps my skin soft. Boy, am I thirsty. It must be over ninety degrees out there.

STEVE / TIM. Here, have a product placement. (*They hand him a Miller Lite.*)

HITCHHIKER. Well, thank you. (*HITCHIKER drinks the entire bottle of beer as everyone else sits and watches.*) Ahhh. That has all the taste but half the calories.

JACK. (*After an uncomfortable beat.*) Let's play a game!

GARY. How about "I Spy"?

HITCHHIKER. I'll start! I spy, with my little eye, something that used to be a slaughterhouse! In the summer, when they'd crank up the bolt guns and fire up them furnaces, you could smell steer guts for twenty square miles if you got lucky and the wind was right. You could hear them cows and hogs squealin', and sometimes it sounded like a person, like a person bein' murdered in cold blood, like a person screamin' for his very own life. Sound like that would stop yer blood cold in yer veins. I know 'cause I heard that very scream myself once, see. It started in the mouth a' someone I was real close to. Someone that got themselves cut ta ribbons right in front a my eyes. And when the screams got closer, and that person gettin' the shit sliced outta himself got done screamin' 'cause he was dead, I realized them screams was comin' from my own mouth. I had a chainsaw diggin' inta my guts, leavin' me with a few scratches— (*He pulls up his shirt to reveal "HORRIBLE SCARS" written on his torso.*)

ALL. (*Horrified screams.*)

HITCHHIKER. (*He puts his shirt back down.*) They say what don't kill ya makes ya stronger, and they're right. I'm stronger now! I can take just about anything. Like this! (*He pulls out a Zima.*)

STEVE / TIM. Oh, my God! He has a Zima!

(*Everyone in the van freaks out as HITCHHIKER chugs the Zima.*)

HITCHHIKER. See? See?! I can take it! You know, you look just like my friend—

(*HITCHIKER grabs JACK and tries to kiss him. ANDREW slams on the brakes. They throw the HITCHHIKER out and speed away. He chases after the car.*)

HITCHHIKER. I can take it! It makes me stronger! But it's gonna kill *you*! Ah ha ha ha ha ha! (*And he's gone.*)

STEVE / TIM. He was dangerous and frightening!

TERRY. Look, there's a diner up ahead. Let's pull over and call the police.

ANDREW. I don't know—

CHUCK. Pull over!

(*CHUCK yanks the wheel to the side. ANDREW stops the van and everyone files out.*)

TERRY. I'll go call the authorities.

JACK. I'm coming with you.

(*They exit. Everyone stretches.*)

ANDREW. You should be careful, Chuck. These babies roll like a donut at high speeds if you jerk the wheel to far.

CHUCK. I imagine the front seat would get pretty trashed in an accident.

ANDREW. Oh, sure. The driver would be meat loaf in a collision.

CHUCK. Then I'll have to try harder next time.

<u>Scene Six</u>

(*CONTINUOUS. JACK and TERRY enter with ROSE, a waitress from the diner, giving directions.*)

ROSE. Well, if you're headin' for that old resort, you're headin' in the right direction. Or the wrong direction, dependin' on how you look at it.

STEVE & TIM. What do you mean?

ROSE. Well, look at you two! Ain't you cute. It's like a Nancy boy version of that Patty Duke show. I bet a hotdog makes you both lose control. (*She cracks herself up.*) Whoo, boy! I just crack my ass!

CHUCK. Did you call the police?

TERRY. No, the diner doesn't have a working telephone.

JACK. And just when we need one. (*Shrugs.*) Oh, well.

ROSE. Sorry 'bout that. I was making calls all morning and afternoon long, and then right before you boys pulled up, poof! Phone died. But don't worry, I'll tell the sheriff all about your run in with that crazy lunatic when I see him. Now, what were we talkin' about before all that exposition?

JACK. The resort.

ROSE. Oh, right, right. The resort. Hard Log Resort. Beautiful place. Two gentlemen bought it in the sixties and fixed it up real nice. Repaintin' and varnishin' and new throw rugs and matchin' curtains. Very El Swankola, if ya know what I mean. Those two, why, they had, well, they had a special knack for decoratin'. Uncanny, it was.

JACK. Why would heading to the resort be the wrong direction?

ROSE. Somethin' terrible happened at Hard Log Resort one year. In fact, exactly twenty years ago this summer, in 1970.

CHUCK. But it's 1984...

ROSE. Somethin' awful. Somethin' unthinkable. Murder. The owner, Richard, caught the other fella with another fella and got crazy mad and took a chainsaw and cut 'em to pieces. At least that's what they think happened. Because they only found one body. When they caught Richard, he wouldn't say a thing. Wouldn't tell them where the other body was, or why he did it, or even his name. All through the trial, he just sat there, starin'. Starin' right through ya if ya happened to catch his gaze. They sent him to the state mental hospital for the rest of his life. Now the worst part of this whole mess is that Hard Log, that nice place for those young men, is cursed. Every time somebody tries openin' that place back up, there's a fire, or someone dies under mysterious circumstances, or the hot water only gets, like, halfway hot.

ALL. (*Improvised "Oh, my God, that's terrible!" reactions.*)

ROSE. Some think it's that fella they never found, that he lived and is makin' damn sure that place never, ever opens again. More than one person swears they saw a man, a horribly scarred man, lurking about in the forest surrounding Hard Log, just waitin' for someone foolish enough to try and reopen it so he can kill 'em off in the same horrible way Richard killed Clifford years before. Maybe so. But this year he's gonna have some help. 'Cause Richard just escaped from that state mental home. And you can just bet he's gonna come straight back here. Back to the forest. Back to his home. To finish off the job he started twenty years ago… (*Big pause.*) So you boys have fun gettin' murdered! Bye! (*She exits.*)

JACK. (*A beat.*) She seems fun.

ANDREW. Back in the van. We're losing light.

(*They clamber back into the van, crank up the music, sit there for a beat, then stop the van and immediately climb back out because they've arrived at—*)

Scene Seven

(*CONTINUOUS. HARD LOG MEN'S RESTORT aka CAMP COMMUNITY MAIN CABIN. Everyone splits up to explore the lodge.*)

JACK. Well, here we are. Camp Community.

CHUCK. More like "Dump" Community.

TERRY. Is that mouse poop? I think that's mouse poop. Hey, look, mouse poop!

STEVE / TIM. This place is disgusting.

CARLOS. (*Entering from kitchen area.*) I just went through the entire contents of the kitchen, and for some reason we're missing an egg beater.

GARY. That seems really specific.

CARLOS. I know, right?

TERRY. Jack, I know this is a good cause and it means a lot to you and all, but they lived better than this on "Land of the Lost."

ANDREW. I loved that show! Remember when they would shove that big log down the dinosaur's throat?

CARLOS. I remember that! And every Saturday morning I'd think, "Lucky dinosaur."

JACK. Alright, I admit this place is a little—

STEVE. Filthy.

TIM. Gross.

TERRY. Squalid.

CARLOS. Disgusting.

GARY. Slimy.

ANDREW. Dank.

CHUCK. Nauseating.

JACK. Shabby. But that's what we're here for. To clean up the cabins. Then next week when the kids get here, it's cake for the rest of the summer.

We just keep them entertained and do our best to make sure they don't drown in the lake while we're having sex for the next two months.

TERRY. Keep them entertained doing what?

JACK. I don't know. Stuff. We'll just play it by ear. Come on. It's just cleaning. It's not gonna kill you.

(*SFX: Spooky music. GARY reveals a theremin which he has just played to make said spooky music.*)

GARY. Look! I found a theremin!

STEVE / TIM. What's a (*Both horribly mispronounce.*) thenererim?

GARY. An electronic musical instrument from 1928. It's named after a Russian inventor named Léon Theremin. You might recognize the sound from the movies, as it has been widely used in soundtracks for suspense films. You play it without touching it, like this. (*Plays the theremin. SFX: Spooky music.*)

TERRY. How perfectly random.

JACK. Okay, I'll go start the generator—

CHUCK. Generator?

JACK. –and then we can get started. We'll be done in no time. I'll be right back.

(*JACK exits as GARY plays the theremin for some spooky exit music.*)

GARY. Cool, huh?

TERRY. He better hurry. It's going to get pretty dark when the sun goes down.

(*The sun abruptly goes down, plunging the cabin into total darkness.*)

TERRY. Uh-oh.

(*GARY plays the theremin which supplies the SFX: Spooky music soundtrack for the KILLER, a hulking figure in coveralls and a hockey mask, as he crosses through the cabin, unseen by the others because of the darkness. He stops center stage and pulls out a horrible weapon with which to terrorize the audience… an egg beater!*)

CHUCK. What was that noise?

STEVE / TIM. Crickets / The wind… (*They look at each other.*) Wind / Crickets…

CHUCK. Didn't sound like crickets to me.

CARLOS. That's just because you're never out in nature.

ANDREW. What did it sound like?

CHUCK. (*Far-away special effects voice of doom:*) Like a hulking murderer in coveralls and a hockey mask carrying a kitchen implement...

(KILLER exits. GARY stops playing the theremin. The lights come back on. JACK enters.)

JACK. I'm back.
CHUCK. Did you see anything out there?
JACK. No. Why?
CARLOS. Jeanne Dixon here thinks the crickets are after him.
CHUCK. Ha ha. I'm busting a gut. Seriously, I think somebody is out there.
JACK. Whatever. Come on, let's put on some music and get this place cleaned up.

(A tape is put into the boom box. SFX: Big Fun Dance Music. The music plays for less than 30 seconds, just enough time for JACK to put up a single set of gaily colored curtains. The music stops.)

JACK. Done!
GARY. Wow!
CARLOS. This place does clean up well.
STEVE. We've got a week before the kids get here.
TIM. What are we gonna do?
JACK. Never fear! I brought, uh, supplies.
ANDREW. Like what?
JACK. Well, I was a camp counselor in high school, so I thought it would be fun if we did the same stuff I did when I was a teenager.
CARLOS. We're gonna stalk and kill a mastodon?
JACK. No. I'm afraid we might accidentally shoot your mother.
ALL. Ooooh...
JACK. So I brought cheap wine...*(Pulls out a bottle of wine.)*
GARY. "Aunt Festa's Boysenberry Ass-Kick"? Jack, this label is hand-written.
JACK. I know!
CARLOS. *(About the label.)* Careful, the tape is coming off.
JACK. And my friend, "Mary Jane." *(Pulls out some pot.)*
ALL. Cool, etc.
ANDREW. There's a girl coming?
CHUCK. Hand me a large rock and I'll put it out of its misery.
JACK. And Trivial Pursuit.
STEVE / TIM. Boring!
TERRY. I never know any of the answers.
JACK. You will this time. It's the new "Laverne & Shirley" edition.
ALL. Okay, great, etc. ...!
CARLOS. But it's still boring. All you do is sit there.

JACK. Not the way I play it.

(*BLACKOUT.*)

Scene Eight

(*LIGHTS UP. Middle of game. Everyone is very stoned and drunk.*)

ANDREW. I have to take a smoke of pot every time I get an answer wrong?
JACK. Every time.
ANDREW. You may not believe this, but I've never smoked grass before. (*He is smoking very badly.*)
CHUCK. No kidding.
ANDREW. Swear.
TERRY. Okay—Fuck!
ALL. (*Improvised hilarity at this. "He said swear, so I did!" "You're a comic genius!" etc.*)
STEVE. Speaking of "fuck"...

(*STEVE and TIM start making out. CARLOS and GARY start making out. TERRY and JACK start making out. ANDREW looks to CHUCK. A beat.*)

CHUCK. Steve, Tim. It's your turn... Hello... Fire... Dolph Lundgren naked...
ALL. Where?!
CHUCK. In my brain. Look, I feel gross from the trip and everything. I'm gonna go out to the bath house and take a shower. Will somebody go out there with me? I'm still nervous about the noises.

(*Everybody looks at each other. Finally...*)

ANDREW. I'll go.
ALL. (*Vehemently.*) Yeah, you go...
CHUCK. Thanks, guys.
ANDREW. Race you there!

(*ANDREW races out.*)

CHUCK. You do that. I'll get you all for this. (*SFX: Thunder crack. He exits.*)
TIM. Come on. I feel like going for a walk by the lake, through the woods we've never been in, in the pitch black darkness.
STEVE. I feel totally safe doing that!

(*TIM and STEVE exit.*)

TERRY. I've got the munchies. Let's go make something to eat.

(*Everyone else exits to the kitchen.*)

Scene Nine

(*FOREST. TIM and STEVE.*)

STEVE. I've got a surprise.
TIM. What?

(*STEVE pulls out a blindfold.*)

TIM. Oooohh…

(*SFX: Scary music.*)

TIM. Wait! Did you hear that?
STEVE. What?
TIM. That scary "Someone Sneaking Up Behind You" music.
STEVE. What? No. It's probably just Gary playing his (*Mispronounced.*) threreritin.
TIM. I swear I heard something. Steve, I'm scared!
STEVE. Well, there's only one thing to do when you're scared in the woods in the middle of nowhere at midnight.
TIM. What?
STEVE. Have sex!
TIM. You're so smart!

(*They start taking off their clothes, putting down a blanket, etc.*)

Scene Ten

(*SPLIT SCENE. BATH HOUSE. ANDREW races in.*)

ANDREW. I win!

(*CHUCK enters.*)

CHUCK. You sure did. Whoopee.
ANDREW. You know, I don't think it's a coincidence that everybody said I should come out here with you.
CHUCK. What?
ANDREW. Swear. I think that those guys are trying to set us up.

CHUCK. No! Really? That's amazing. That thought never crossed my mind.
ANDREW. Never?
CHUCK. Never.
ANDREW. Oh. Okay. Well, anyway, time for a shower.

(*SFX: Funky 80's music starts. Spotlight on ANDREW, who is suddenly a stripper with killer moves. As he strips naked, ANDREW is revealed to be totally hot underneath that dork exterior. CHUCK is agog. After the strip, lights restore.*)

ANDREW. (*Still a nerd, even though he's hot and naked.*) Race you to the stalls!

(*He exits to showers. CHUCK starts yanking off his clothes.*)

ANDREW. (*Off.*) Hey! There aren't any stalls, just one big room!
CHUCK. Don't use all the hot water!

(*Naked, CHUCK exits to showers.*)

Scene Eleven

(*FOREST. STEVE is in his underwear, TIM is naked except for his boots.*)

STEVE. Why are you still wearing your boots?
TIM. I don't want to step in anything. Look, there's deer poop!
STEVE. That's not poop, it's… a rock. See? It's hard.
TIM. Well, we can't let that be the only thing hard out here.

(*SFX: Having Sex music. They start to go at it.*)

STEVE. Shit! I forgot the condoms! Well, don't worry. I won't cum in you.

(*SFX: Having Sex music abruptly stops.*)

TIM. Don't worry? Steve, having unprotected sex is irresponsible behavior!

(*SFX: Scary music.*)

TIM. Wait! There it is again! That "Maniac On The Loose" music!
STEVE. Don't worry, it's just Gary's (*Mispronounce.*) therberiflim.
TIM. Don't worry? Steve, ignoring scary music in the woods is irresponsible behavior!

STEVE. Alright, alright. Here, you put on this blindfold, and I'll go get the condoms and check the area for strangers. Okay?
TIM. Okay.

(*They smooch. STEVE exits. TIM puts on his blindfold. SFX: Scary music. KILLER enters, grabs TIM and forces him to his knees.*)

TIM. Steve, is that you? Steve, you're scaring me!

(*KILLER turns his back to audience, standing in front of TIM. We hear SFX: zzzzip.*)

TIM. Now there's a sound I like!

(*KILLER grabs TIM's head and forces it down onto his dick. He is strangling TIM. Finally TIM falls to the ground, dead. The KILLER exits. STEVE enters.*)

STEVE. I'm back. Got the condoms. And there's nobody around for miles. Boy, do you look relaxed…

(*He climbs on top of TIM and starts kissing him. When TIM doesn't move, STEVE realizes he is dead. With a scream he leaps to his feet. The KILLER enters with a spatula.*)

STEVE. Oh, my God!

(*STEVE runs away. KILLER slowly walks off in the other direction.*)

Scene Twelve

(*BATH HOUSE. CHUCK and ANDREW enter, drying off post-shower.*)

ANDREW. Weird how all the shower heads were broken so we had to share the same one, huh?
CHUCK. Mystifying, truly.

(*STEVE screams offstage.*)

ANDREW. Those crickets are loud!
CHUCK. No, that sounded like a scream!
ANDREW. We better get dressed and get back to the main cabin!
CHUCK. No! We don't have time to change! We must stay in these skimpy towels and race back to the others!
ANDREW. Oh, okay.

CHUCK. Crickets my ass…

(*They exit.*)

Scene Thirteen

(*MAIN CABIN. TERRY, JACK, CARLOS and GARY eat heinous, stoner food.*)

JACK. Okay, try this. Deluxe Grahams dipped in French onion dip.

(*They all try it and, surprise, surprise, it tastes great!*)

ALL. Delicious, yum, who knew…? Etc.
GARY. Okay, I got one. Vienna sausages in jam.

(*They are just about to try this when STEVE bursts in, hysterical. He is now naked.*)

STEVE. Thank God! (*Passes out.*)

(*CHUCK and ANDREW enter.*)

CHUCK. What's going on?
CARLOS. Tim, what's wrong? Where's Steve?
TERRY. That is Steve.
CARLOS. Is it?
JACK. I think it's Tim.
CHUCK. I think it's Steve, but I've never really known the difference.
CARLOS. Did either of them have some sort of distinguishing birthmark or something?
JACK. Oh! Yes, one of them had a mole right about his ass. I remember from that four-way tag team we had with them.
TERRY. Flip him over.

(*They flip STEVE over so his ass is showing. There is a mole above one butt cheek.*)

JACK. There it is!
TERRY. Mystery solved.
JACK. Except I can't remember which one had the mole.

(*STEVE regains consciousness.*)

STEVE. Uhh….

CHUCK. Hey...you. Are you okay?

ANDREW. Why are you naked?

STEVE. As I was running through the forest, the branches kept catching my underwear and slowing me down, so I was forced to take them off.

GARY. Running? From what?

STEVE. ...naked... boots... condoms... death... spatula... (*Faints.*)

ANDREW. You're not supposed to talk during charades.

JACK. Spatula? What does he mean by spatula?

CARLOS. It was the sled. (*After a confused beat.*) "Citizen Kane?"

CHUCK. "Rosebud," you idiot.

(*TERRY has examined STEVE.*)

TERRY. We better go find Tim and/or Steve. Jack, you come with me. The rest of you stay here. Don't mess with Steve or Tim, he's in shock. Don't leave the cabin until we come back and figure out what's going on. Don't unlock the door. Don't run with scissors, don't sleep in the subway, don't look in the basement, don't tell me how to live and putter... (*He and JACK crack up.*) We're so stoned!

(*TERRY and JACK exit.*)

CARLOS. Now what?

ANDREW. Maybe we should put some clothes on him.

CHUCK. No! He's in a state of shock. Like Terry said, he must remain naked until he regains consciousness. We can't touch him. We just have to wait.

(*They all stare at STEVE's prone, naked body.*)

Scene Fourteen

(*WOODS. TERRY and JACK come across TIM's body.*)

JACK. Oh, my God! Terry, look! It's Steve or Tim!

TERRY. He's dead.

JACK. How?!

TERRY. (*He examines the body.*) Well, judging from these lacerations on his mouth and face, I would say he choked to death on a huge penis.

JACK. (*A beat.*) At least he didn't suffer.

TERRY. Let's take his body back to the cabin.

JACK. Yuck!

TERRY. Jack!

JACK. He's all dead and stuff. Gross!

TERRY. Listen, mister. Steve or Tim was your friend. You've been through a lot together. Remember how you and I first met? We were spit roasting him and/or the other one at a sex party, and spontaneously high fived over him or the other one right before we ejaculated, and you said, "Look! We're making the Eiffel Tower!" You don't get many truly good friends in life, and now that you've lost one, I'd think you'd want him to lie with dignity instead of out here in the middle of the woods. He loved you like a brother that you fuck every now and then, and I know you felt the same way about him. And I'm certain he wouldn't leave you out here like this. Right?

JACK. I guess...

TERRY. Good. Now help me drag his dead carcass back to the cabin.

(*They pick up TIM and carry him off.*)

Scene Fifteen

(*MAIN CABIN. GARY, CARLOS, CHUCK and ANDREW still stare at STEVE's unconscious body.*)

GARY. We can't stand here all night.

CARLOS. Oh, I don't know...

GARY. I have to go to the bathroom.

CARLOS. It's a previously unmentioned plot device that all the toilets are in the bath house, not the main cabin. You'll just have to wait.

GARY. But I really have to go!

CHUCK. We can't split up, it's not safe. Just step outside and pee and then come right back in.

CARLOS. Here we go...

GARY. I can't go outside. I have nature pee-fright.

CHUCK / ANDREW. What?

GARY. I can't go to the bathroom outdoors. If I whip it out outside, some crazed boar could bite it off, or a wasp might land on it or something.

ANDREW. Don't forget rattlesnakes.

CHUCK. Well, it looks like you've got this particular neurosis all mapped out, so what are you gonna do? We have to stay together until those guys get back.

GARY. (*Thinks for a moment.*) Anyone here a piss bottom?

CHUCK. You can pee in someone's mouth, but you can't pee outside?

GARY. I use fantasy so it's not like I'm just peeing on someone's face. I pretend their face is a toilet that can talk and likes to choke on my urine.

CHUCK. You're going to make a great father some day.

GARY. Carlos, come with me to the bath house.

CARLOS. I don't know...

GARY. We'll be fine. We'll just run out and run right back. Please!

ANDREW. You guys!

CARLOS. Okay, but let's make this quick. We'll be right back.

(*They exit.*)

CHUCK. Shit!

(*As CHUCK and ANDREW wait inside, KILLER crosses outside with a rolling pin. SFX: Scary music. Back inside:*)

ANDREW. Chuck, I'm frightened.
CHUCK. Come here. Let me comfort you over the body of our comatose friend.

(*The comforting progresses to making out over STEVE's body. TERRY and JACK enter with TIM's body. CHUCK sees them.*)

CHUCK. Fuck!
ANDREW. Alright! (*He flips CHUCK onto his back.*)
TERRY. You guys, help us with Tim or Steve's body.
CHUCK. My God!
ANDREW. What happened?
TERRY. He choked to death on a huge penis.
CHUCK. Well, at least he died doing what he loved.

(*TIM's body has been set down beside STEVE.*)

TERRY. Let's move some stuff in the bedroom so we can put the body in there.

(*The four of them exit into bedroom. STEVE wakes up and sees TIM. He has forgotten that TIM is dead.*)

STEVE. Oh, Tim. I just had the worst dream. A spatula-wielding maniac had killed you and—

(*He realizes TIM is indeed dead, screams and passes out again. TERRY, JACK, ANDREW and CHUCK enter, oblivious to STEVE's scream.*)

TERRY. Help me carry him in.

(*They pick up TIM and exit.*)

Scene Sixteen

(*WOODS. CARLOS and GARY. GARY comes out of the bath house.*)

CARLOS. Better?

GARY. Much.

CARLOS. Good. Now let's get back to the others.

GARY. Or...

CARLOS. What?

GARY. We could have sex!

CARLOS. Steven or Tim is in shock, Tim or Steve is dead, and there's probably some evil, disfigured, hulking serial killer skulking around in the woods. As always your timing is perfect!

(*They get all naked and begin having sex. SPLIT FOCUS with MAIN CABIN and WOODS.*)

ANDREW. What are we gonna do?

TERRY. We'll wait for Carlos and Gary, then take the van and get out of here.

(*The KILLER enters the woods as CARLOS and GARY make love. He sneaks up behind them and stabs them with his rolling pin, pinning them together. In the main cabin the guys hear CARLOS and GARY's screams as they die.*)

TERRY. Pack it up!

(*They start gathering their belongings.*)

ANDREW. I'll go start the van.

CHUCK. Wait! You can't go out there unarmed.

ANDREW. You're right. What do we have?

(*JACK goes through one of their bags.*)

JACK. Let's see—firewood axe, pistol, butcher knife, sledgehammer, and Silly String.

ANDREW. Great. I'll take this and be right back. (*Takes the Silly String.*)

CHUCK. Wait! Before you go—

(*He grabs ANDREW and kisses him, hard. Finally the others have to pull them apart.*)

ANDREW. Bye! (*Exits.*)

TERRY. Come on. Let's get packed.

(*Everyone starts packing.*)

Scene Seventeen

(*WOODS. ANDREW makes his way through the trees to the van. He gets in and tries to start it, but the engine won't turn over.*)

ANDREW. Rats!

(*He gets out of the van and opens the hood. The KILLER appears an electric beater with an extension cord trailing off stage to supply power. ANDREW backs up from the car and sees the KILLER.*)

ANDREW. Oh, shit...

(*The KILLER attacks him and they do battle. ANDREW fights valiantly with the Silly String. At some point the electric beater comes unplugged and the KILLER signals "Just a minute," goes off and plugs it back in, then resumes murdering ANDREW. ANDREW manages to overpower the KILLER by wrapping the extension cord around his neck and strangling him to death. Or does he? ANDREW cautiously approaches the KILLER's body to check it for signs of life. The KILLER springs up and, using one of the beaters, kills ANDREW. The KILLER exits, leaving the electric beater behind.*)

Scene Eighteen

(*MAIN CABIN. Everything is packed.*)

JACK. All set.
TERRY. Okay, Chuck, help Steve or Tim and let's get the hell out of here.

(*They exit the cabin and enter the WOODS. As they make their way to the van, CHUCK spies the electric beater.*)

CHUCK. Oh, my God! He's dead! Andrew's dead!
TERRY. That's not Andrew, that's an electric beater.
CHUCK. Right. Sorry. My mistake. (*Spies ANDREW's dead body.*) Oh, my God! He's dead! (*Unceremoniously dumps STEVE on the ground and runs over to ANDREW's body and points to it.*) It's really him this time!
TERRY. Oh. Okay.
CHUCK. Why? Why? We never should have let him go out alone. He was just a kid. A boy, really. A young man ready to taste all that had been set before him on an "all you can eat" buffet of life. Ready to do a little dance, make a little love, get down tonight. A candle in the wind who'd

made it through the rain and looked at love from both sides now. Sweet dreams are made of these, and I would be a lesser man if I were to disagree. And to top it off, I loved him. I honestly loved him. He lit up my life. And now? Now, he's walking up that stairway to heaven. Oh, my undercover angel, my midnight fantasy, tonight's the night they killed an innocent man. If only you'd da doo run... *run*! Well Mr. Maniacal Killer, his boyfriend is back, and you're gonna be in trouble! His boyfriend is *back*, smart guy, so you had better get out on the double! I won't get no satisfaction until my finger is on the trigger shootin' at the walls of heartache - Bang! Bang! I am the warrior!

(*TERRY, JACK, STEVE [sitting up from unconsciousness], ANDREW [sitting up from death] and hopefully the audience applaud furiously. CHUCK is handed a bouquet of roses. CHUCK acknowledges this modestly.*)

TERRY. That was beautiful. Now roll his dead body into that ditch and let's get the fuck out of here.

(*They roll ANDREW's body off while JACK checks the van.*)

JACK. The van is ruined! Someone pulled out all these wires or something.
CHUCK. Can't we fix it?
JACK. We're gay men in the 80s. Our onscreen portrayals still perpetuate the myth we don't know anything about cars.
CHUCK. Oh. Right. So what are we gonna do now?

(*The three argue with their backs to STEVE. As they fight, the KILLER enters with a plunger. He kills STEVE, unnoticed by the others, by plunging his face until his heart is sucked out of his mouth.*)

JACK. I don't know.
CHUCK. Well, you better figure it out soon, genius, because you got us into this mess.
JACK. Hey! Nobody forced you to come. In fact, I wish you would have stayed home. At least then I'd die at the hands of a psycho-killer in peace!
TERRY. You guys! Come on!
CHUCK. (*Mocking.*) It'll be fun. It's for a good cause. Yeah, good cause—an organ donor bank!
JACK. Well, I can think of one organ that would be thrown out. "We can't use this one, Doctor. It's atrophied from lack of use!"
CHUCK. (*Spooky reverb voice.*) I knew something bad was—
JACK. And cut that shit out! Mr. Psychic Connection. How about you use this "gift" to warn us before someone gets killed.

CHUCK. It's a contrivance! It doesn't work that way!

TERRY. That's enough! It doesn't matter whose fault all this is. We have to pull it together and figure out a way to get out of here before it's too late. Now help me get whatshisname—

(*They notice STEVE for the first time.*)

TERRY. We've got to start paying more attention.

CHUCK. What happened?

TERRY. His heart was sucked out of his mouth with a plunger.

JACK. He had a plunger on his *mouth*?!

JACK / CHUCK. Sick!

TERRY. Come on.

(*We hear a stick snap.*)

CHUCK. What was that?

(*We hear rustling in the bushes. Then an animal-like growling joins in. Then a chainsaw buzz. Then horrible screams. All the sounds get louder and closer.*)

JACK. Shit! He's coming!

(*Just as the sounds reach their peak, ROSE enters.*)

TERRY / JACK / CHUCK. Rose!

ROSE. Hi, fellas! Sorry about the noise. I tripped over a sack of soda cans. Damn campers! Leavin' their trash from Hell to breakfast.

TERRY. Rose, do you have a car? We need to get back to town immediately!

ROSE. What? No. Well, yes, but it broke down about a mile from here. I thought I'd stop by and see how you boys was doin' and ended up takin' a hike through them woods. (*She sees the dead bodies.*) Oh, my Lord! What happened here?

CHUCK. He's dead! And everyone else, too! We're the only ones left!

ROSE. Dead? All those beautiful men, dead?

JACK. And the killer is still loose.

ROSE. I knew it! This camp never shoulda been reopened!

TERRY. The main cabin is the safest place right now. Let's take these bodies back to the cabin and barricade ourselves in.

CHUCK. Why do we have to keep bringing the bodies back to the cabin? They're dead.

ROSE. You don't want some rabid wolf takin' a chomp outta your nice dead friend's face, do ya?

CHUCK. Uh, I guess not…

ROSE. Then move your tuckus. 1, 2, 3, lift... (*Too heavy.*) Let's just roll it into the ditch.

(*They roll STEVE's body off stage then make their way back into the cabin.*)

Scene Nineteen

(*MAIN CABIN.*)

JACK. We better barricade ourselves in. (*He leans a broom against the door.*) Much better.

CHUCK. For now, but what next? Nobody is supposed to be here for almost a week. We can't stay locked inside for six days.

JACK. Says who? If it's a choice between that or being eviscerated with some kitchen appliance, I'll stay inside for as long as it takes.

ROSE. Speakin' of kitchen appliances, I think I'll check out the mess area. (*Exits to kitchen.*)

JACK. It's boiling in here.

TERRY. Let's get rid of these clothes.

(*JACK and TERRY strip down to their jockstraps.*)

CHUCK. Is it really necessary for you to be in your jockstraps right now?

TERRY. Hey, who's the dentist here?

CHUCK. What?

TERRY. If it gets too hot, we might develop heat prostration and then be unable to defend ourselves.

CHUCK. Ah.

TERRY. Maybe we should come up with a plan to get help, or make weapons from things in the house so we can defend ourselves.

JACK. Or we could play a game! Twenty Questions? I'll think of some celebrity and you get twenty questions to guess. Okay?

TERRY. Sure.

JACK. Okay, got one. Chuck, you start.

CHUCK. (*Spooky reverb voice.*) Is it Ruth Buzzi?

JACK. (*Pissed.*) No.

CHUCK. Really? Wow. I'm usually pretty good about those things. Is it a woman who—

JACK. Alright, yes! It's Ruth Buzzi! Fucking A! I am so sick of your brain.

CHUCK. Jack, I'm sorry. Go again and I won't use my brain.

(*SFX: window breaking from the kitchen.*)

TERRY. Rose!

(They race offstage to the kitchen, then immediately race back onstage.)

CHUCK. She's gone!

JACK. He's got her!

CHUCK. We gotta go get her!

TERRY. We can't go get her, 'cause he's got her, and if he's got her, then she's a goner!

JACK. Terry!

TERRY. Be realistic, you idiots! He killed everybody else here. I don't think he's interested in taking hostages at this point. *(The lights go out.)* Shit!

CHUCK. The lights are out all over the camp. He must have shut off the generator.

JACK. We've got to have light! Our only defense is being able to see him coming.

CHUCK. Alright, I'm going to go out and fix the generator.

JACK. You?!

CHUCK. Yes! Me! We need light or we're dead for sure. I'll go because if he gets me, at least it won't break up a couple. I'd hate to live with the one of you that has to live without the other. You were both terrible people when you were single.

JACK. *(Taking CHUCK's hand.)* You are a true friend.

TERRY. Chuck, let's all go.

CHUCK. No! You stay here and re-barricade the door when I leave. At least you'll have the walls to protect you. Besides, we could all get separated in the woods anyway.

(TERRY and JACK both give CHUCK a big hug and kiss.)

TERRY. Take care, Chuck.

JACK. And come back.

CHUCK. I'll try. *(He takes the broom from the door and opens it.)* Put this back when I leave, and don't open this door for anyone until I get back.

JACK. Okay.

(CHUCK exits the door, the pops his head back in.)

CHUCK. Neither of you was, by chance, going to try and stop me from going? Like physically, or anything?

TERRY / JACK. No.

CHUCK. Shit.

(CHUCK exits, and they prop the broom back against the door.)

JACK. We're never going to see him again.

TERRY. I think you're right.

JACK. You know, you were real sexy when you got all mad when we wanted to go save Rose.

TERRY. Really?

JACK. Yeah. Like when you said, all forceful like, "We can't go get her, 'cause he's got her, and if he's got her, then she's a goner!"

TERRY. We can't go get her, 'cause he's got her, and if he's got her, then she's a goner!

JACK. Yeah! Just like that. Do more. Convince me that it's hopeless to try and save somebody, with alliteration.

TERRY. Um... He's getting her good, and her guts are all gory!

JACK. Yes!

TERRY. He'll stick her and stab her with scissors and a stapler...

(*JACK, totally turned on, makes the moves on TERRY, who is also finding this game very sexy.*)

JACK. More!

TERRY. More, shit! She sells sea shells by the sea shore!

(*And by now they have taken off what is left of their clothes and do what all people being stalked by a maniac do: have sex. SPLIT SCENE with GENERATOR. CHUCK has made it to the power house.*)

CHUCK. Great. Now what?

(*He fiddles with the generator. In MAIN CABIN JACK and TERRY continue having sex as the KILLER tries to open the door, but can't because of the broom.*)

TERRY. What was that?

JACK. It's a new thing I'm trying with my tongue. I read about it in Blueboy Magazine.

TERRY. No, the other that. (*Reacts to the door again.*) That that.

JACK. Whatever it is, is it more important than me going down on you?

TERRY. Absolutely not.

(*JACK and TERRY continue having sex. The KILLER enters the MAIN CABIN through a window. He is carrying a melon scoop. He grabs TERRY by the hair and lifts him off JACK and cuts his throat with the scoop. Blood flies everywhere. JACK scrambles and tries to get away. The KILLER grabs him and kills him with a wisk.*

At the GENERATOR. Chuck has heard the screams from the main cabin.)

CHUCK. Fuck! No!

(He exits the GENERATOR house and runs into the:)

Scene Twenty

(WOODS. CHUCK runs toward the main cabin but is stopped short by the KILLER, who has an ice cube tray. CHUCK screams.)

CHUCK. Aiiiieeee!

(And runs. He and the KILLER run in place as if participating in a great chase scene; CHUCK fast, the KILLER lumbering but keeping up with him. In running, CHUCK trips, allowing the KILLER to get closer. CHUCK regains his footing and runs again... with a limp, of course. Finally CHUCK makes it to the MAIN CABIN. He can't get in the door because of the broom, so he goes around and climbs in the window. As he climbs in, he bumps his head on the sill and momentarily falls to the ground. There is a corresponding LIGHT CHANGE. Suddenly, the HITCHHIKER appears in the window.)

HITCHHIKER. Aha!
CHUCK. Shit!

(HITCHHIKER enters through the window.)

HITCHHIKER. So. Ya found my little home away from home.
CHUCK. Your home?
HITCHHIKER. Yeah. I spent a little time at Hard Log Men's Resort about twenty years ago.
CHUCK. In 1964?
HITCHHIKER. No! 1970. Twenty years ago.
CHUCK. Seriously, can no one do math around here?

(He advances on CHUCK, but both of them are stopped in their tracks by inhuman noises from outside.)

CHUCK. What's that?
HITCHHIKER. My guess would be the toxic waste from that nearby nuclear power plant has caused the dead to rise from the grave in search of living flesh to satiate their cannibalistic hunger.
CHUCK. What? You're nuts!

(All of the dead counselors—STEVE, TIM, CARLOS, GARY, JACK, TERRY, and ANDREW—appear at the window.)

ANDREW. Hey, Chuck, look!

STEVE / TIM. We're the undead!

(*They try to get through the window all at once.*)

TERRY. Hey, quit pushing!
CARLOS. I'm not pushing. Gary, honey, make them let me eat the crazed hitchhiker lunatic first.
GARY. You know, *we* were killed first --
STEVE / TIM. Nuh uh!

(*They all start bickering. TERRY finally puts a stop to the fight.*)

TERRY. Hey! You guys! (*He indicates to the HITCHHIKER.*)
ALL. Oh, right, etc....

(*And they all stream in and drag the HITCHHIKER away screaming. CHUCK faints dead away in the very same spot he fell to the floor when he bumped his head. Suddenly he jerks awake, and by the LIGHT CHANGE we know what just happened was a hallucination.*)

CHUCK. It was all a dream. A well-timed dream.

(*Bang bang bang! A knock on the door.*)

RICHARD. (*Off.*) Hey! You alright in there?
CHUCK. Hello?!
RICHARD. (*Off.*) I saw two guys stabbed with a rolling pin up the road. I came to help.
CHUCK. Thank God!
(*CHUCK removes the broom from the door. RICHARD enters. He looks much older, and should be wearing gloves with whatever costume he has on.*)

RICHARD. Are you okay?
CHUCK. I think so. Look, we've got to get help. Everybody here at the camp has been murdered by some maniac. I'm the only one left. Please! You've got to help me!
RICHARD. Calm down, son, calm down. I think we should stay here, at least for the night.
CHUCK. What? Are you crazy?
RICHARD. Now son, there's more going on than just your friends being murdered in this area tonight. A couple was attacked in their car just up the road a bit.
CHUCK. What happened?
RICHARD. Two young men were in their car on a deserted stretch of

Highway 58 earlier this evening. Apparently they had pulled over and were in a state of undress, expressing their youthful passions as young men are wont to do in this area of the wilderness. At that exact moment, over the radio comes a report of an escaped lunatic from the state mental institution. This unnamed patient had spent the better part of the last twenty years in maximum security rehab. And instead of his hand, he had a hook. Anyway, just as this piece of information comes out of the radio, these two young men hear a "metal against metal" sound, like somebody trying to open the back door with a pipe or crowbar. Thinking fast, the young man at the wheel speeds away, and doesn't stop until he reaches the police station almost ten miles down the road. When they step outside of the car, they discover, dangling from the back door handle, a shiny metal hook. The police still haven't caught the owner of that hook. An owner which, I'm sure, is very angry at the loss of that hook.

CHUCK. What horrible crime did he commit?

RICHARD. Actually it was right here, in this very room. Murder. Manslaughter. Justifiable homicide.

CHUCK. Justifiable—

RICHARD. Yes, you see, I caught them fooling around. Just like I caught those two young men in the car fooling around. Just like I caught those young men in the forest fooling around, and without a condom, those bad boys. In this day and age.

CHUCK. You—

RICHARD. Yes, me. And now since I've caught *you* fooling around, I'm going to have to use this— (*He pulls off his glove to reveal a garlic press.*)

CHUCK. (*Combo scream/speak.*) Aaiiiiieeeeewait a minute! That's a garlic press.

RICHARD. I know that. Weren't you paying attention to the story? The hook came off on the car door.

CHUCK. Why didn't you get another hook?

RICHARD. What? You think you can just go buy a hook at Walgreen's? No. I had to make do with what I had in my knapsack. Now stop squirming. You'll just make this worse—

(*The KILLER enters, carrying an ice cube tray.*)

CHUCK. Oh, thank God you're back! This other serial killer was trying to kill me!

(*The KILLER grabs RICHARD and they struggle, ending up outside. We hear RICHARD being killed. In the meantime, CHUCK has closed the door and replaced the broom. The KILLER is outside. We can hear him. CHUCK searches for a weapon, cataloguing what's in the room.*)

CHUCK. Fireplace poker. Logs. Deer head mounted on the wall with sharp antlers. Dammit, is there nothing here I can use as a weapon?! Waitaminute!

(Suddenly seized with an inspiration, he runs into the kitchen and returns with a popsicle. He quickly eats it, stopping midway to have a brain freeze. Left with a bare popsicle stick, he sharpens it by rubbing it on the ground. The KILLER tries the door and can't get in because of the broom. He moves to the window and becomes impossibly tangled in the curtains.)

CHUCK. Come on, you motherfucker! I got a popsicle stick sharpened to a fine point, and I'm not afraid to use it!

(The KILLER finally enters. He and CHUCK face off.)

CHUCK. Okay! Okay! Obviously you can kill me. You've got an ice cube tray and all I've got is this sharpened stick.
KILLER. Grrrrrr…
CHUCK. Wait! Wait! Wait! Okay, you're gonna kill me. But aren't you supposed to reveal yourself to the last victim so we can find out who the killer really is?
KILLER. But—
CHUCK. No, no buts, mister! Fair is fair! You've murdered all my friends, so the least you can do is reveal to me your true identity.
KILLER. But… I… Fuck. Alright.

(The KILLER takes off his mask, to be revealed as—)

CHUCK. Rose!
ROSE. In the flesh! Hi, honey! You know, you're good at this. You made it until the very last. And ya know, I'm glad you made me take off that mask. It's turnin' my powder base into a flaky crust.
CHUCK. But why?
ROSE. Huh? What? Oh, right, right, right. Now's where I got this big, long-ass monologue to explain why I'm killin' all you kids and tryin' to keep this camp closed. Okay, well, it… Ya know what? Guess.
CHUCK. Oh. Okay. Ummm…You're the child of one of the men involved in that incident twenty years ago, bent on revenge?
ROSE. Nope.
CHUCK. You're a psychopathic, bisexual cross-dresser?
ROSE. Hah! Right! I admit this pair of overalls ain't too form fittin', but these babies *(Indicates her breasts.)* is all woman.
CHUCK. You're the former lover or wife of a man who turned out to be gay, wreaking vengeance?

ROSE. Lord, no! What I said about homosexuals in my first monologue was true. They're just peachy.

CHUCK. Then what?! What are your motives?

ROSE. I'm just nuts! Ain't that a kick in the snatch? I'm killin' people 'cause I'm crazy as a loon! Whee! It's Rose's turn!

CHUCK. No!

(ROSE attacks CHUCK. They have a huge battle, much rolling around, punching, etc. Feel free to be creative and ridiculous with the fight choreography. Finally they fall together with the ice cube tray between them, struggling.)

CHUCK. I can't let you live! Even if it means killing myself! Must... use... psychic... powers... foreshadowed in beginning of play... to... cause... house to collapse...

ROSE. Nooooo!!!!

(BLACKOUT. SFX: House collapsing. VIDEO of general comic destruction. Video ends.)

Scene Twenty-One

(MAIN CABIN. The next morning. CHUCK lies motionless on the floor. There is no sign of ROSE. TWO COPS enter.)

COP ONE. Holy crap! This place has been destroyed by some unholy force! There's another one!

COP TWO. I didn't think it could get any worse than those two stuck together with the rolling pin.

COP ONE. Shit! There's more in here! *(He indicates the bedroom.)*

COP TWO. Good thing we got that tip off about those safety violations or we might have had a whole camp filled with dead teenagers in about a week.

(CHUCK groans and moves.)

COP TWO. Hey, look! We got a live one!

COP ONE. Just lie still, son. We'll have an ambulance here in no time.

CHUCK. The waitress... the waitress...

COP ONE. What?

CHUCK. Rose... the waitress... from town...

COP TWO. Rose? Waitress? There ain't no waitress named Rose in town.

CHUCK. She was here. She did all this. She killed everyone. You've got to find her!

COP ONE. Calm down, son. You're gonna be fine.

COP TWO. He don't need no ambulance. He needs a padded cell.

CHUCK. (*Stunned.*) The waitress... you've got to find the waitress... Rose... bud. (*Passes out.*)

(*ROSE's laugh echoes through the air as we BLACKOUT.*)

THE END?

OTHER PLAYS BY THIS AUTHOR FROM PLAYS TO ORDER

Horrible Shakespeare:
A Mini Musical

Book/lyrics by Sean Abley, Music/lyrics by Ryan O'Connell

Musical One-Act, 30 minutes
Cast - 21 either

A student field trip to Shakespeare's Globe Theatre in London takes a horrible turn. In this 30-minute musical, a nameless tour guide leads the students into the sub-sub-sub basement of the theater, which houses the Horrible Productions of Shakespeare's Plays Museum. Each exhibit magically transports the tour into a truly wretched production of some of Shakespeare's most famous works - "Romeo Mime vs. Clown Juliet," "Santa Hamlet," "Macbeth's Burgers," "Taming of the Real, Live Shrew" and "Twelfth Night of the Living Dead."

Perfect for festivals with time restrictions, in-class performances, or as one half of an evening of one-acts. Sheet music, demo tracks and performance karaoke tracks also available.

ABOUT THE PLAYWRIGHT

Sean Abley was born and raised in Helena, MT. After a stint in the theater department at the University of Montana, he moved to Chicago where he cofounded the Factory Theater. While there, he wrote, directed and appeared in over 20 shows, including *Attack Of The Killer B's* (Backstage West Garland Award for the L.A. restaging), *Reefer Madness* (non-musical version), *Bitches, Santa Claus Conquers The Martians: The Musical, Nuclear Family, Corpse Grinders*, and *P*. After moving to Los Angeles, Sean's playwriting career continued to flourish, with hundreds of productions of his two dozen-plus plays all across the U.S. and around the world including the musicals *Welcome to the Afterlife!* and *Horror High: The Musical*; the comedies *The Adventures Of Rose Red* (*Snow White's Less-Famous Sister*), *The End Of The World* (*With Prom To Follow*), and *Dr. Frankincense And The Christmas Monster*; an ever increasing number of plays for high school actors; and the decidedly adult fare *L.A. Tool and Die: Live!*

A staff writing job on the *You Don't Know Jack* cd-rom series opened the doors to scripted television, with multiple episodes of *So Weird* (Disney Channel), *Sabrina – The Animated Series* (ABC), *Digimon* (Fox Kids) and *Mega Babies* (Fox Kids); pilots for MTV and Voxxy.com; and several animated pilots for Klasky-Csupo including *Turbo Snail, Schmutz*, and *Bench Pressly And Sho-Girl* (with Ahmet Zappa, starring Bruce Campbell and Tim Curry). In the "Where exactly does this fit in?" category, Sean also wrote the scripted material for the *Men In Black: Alien Attack* theme park attraction at Universal Studios Florida.